GLADYS KALICHINI

...THESE GESTURES OF MEMORY

KÜNSTLERHAUS BETHANIEN KFW STIFTUNG

Preface

The residency of Zambian artist and researcher Gladys Kalichini at Künstlerhaus Bethanien coincided with the global outbreak of the Coronavirus. Not only has the pandemic brought the international art world to a standstill, but it has also starkly revealed the structural conditions underlying artistic production today. The radical curtailment of worldwide mobility has dealt a heavy blow to the entire art scene since constant travelling is an established pillar of our contemporary cultural and intellectual world. Journeys of all kinds, personal encounters or the experience of new cities and landscapes together contribute to our understanding of different systems of knowledge. They each broaden and open our minds. In light of our new perspective, essential interactions such as these have gained even more significance. As a result, both the mission and potential of international residencies as facilitators for cultural creation and intellectual exchange stand out once again. KfW Stiftung in cooperation with Künstlerhaus Bethanien offers to up-and-coming visual artists such a journey of encounter and experience in Berlin. During year-long residencies, artists are given the time and space to develop their creative projects. These are subsequently showcased in an exhibition and captured in a monographic catalogue. This edition of the ongoing publication series provides an extensive insight into the current work of Gladys Kalichini. Drawing largely on archival material, the artist investigates the historical role of female freedom fighters in the struggles before and after Zambian and Zimbabwean independence in the 1960s and 1980s respectively. Her artworks – often large-scale textile installations – address the fact that many of these women and their achievements do not feature in their respective countries' public culture of remembrance, nor in their national narratives and storytelling. Kalichini's artwork is monumental in both scale and import: it raises questions of collective mourning and in this way suggests alternative perspectives on the female role in collective memory, historiography and oral culture.

Daniela Leykam and Christoph Tannert
Editors

Contents

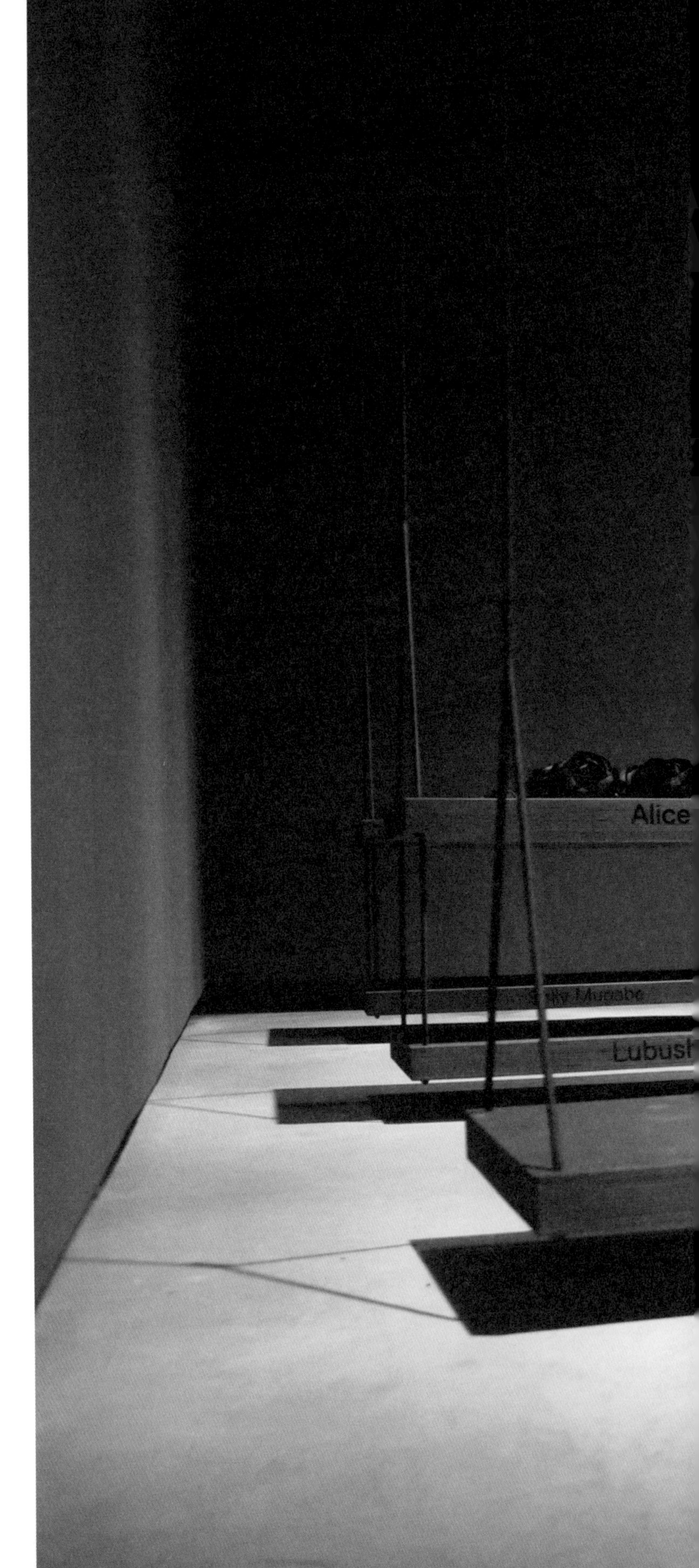

...these wreaths are laid in honour of her memories, 2020

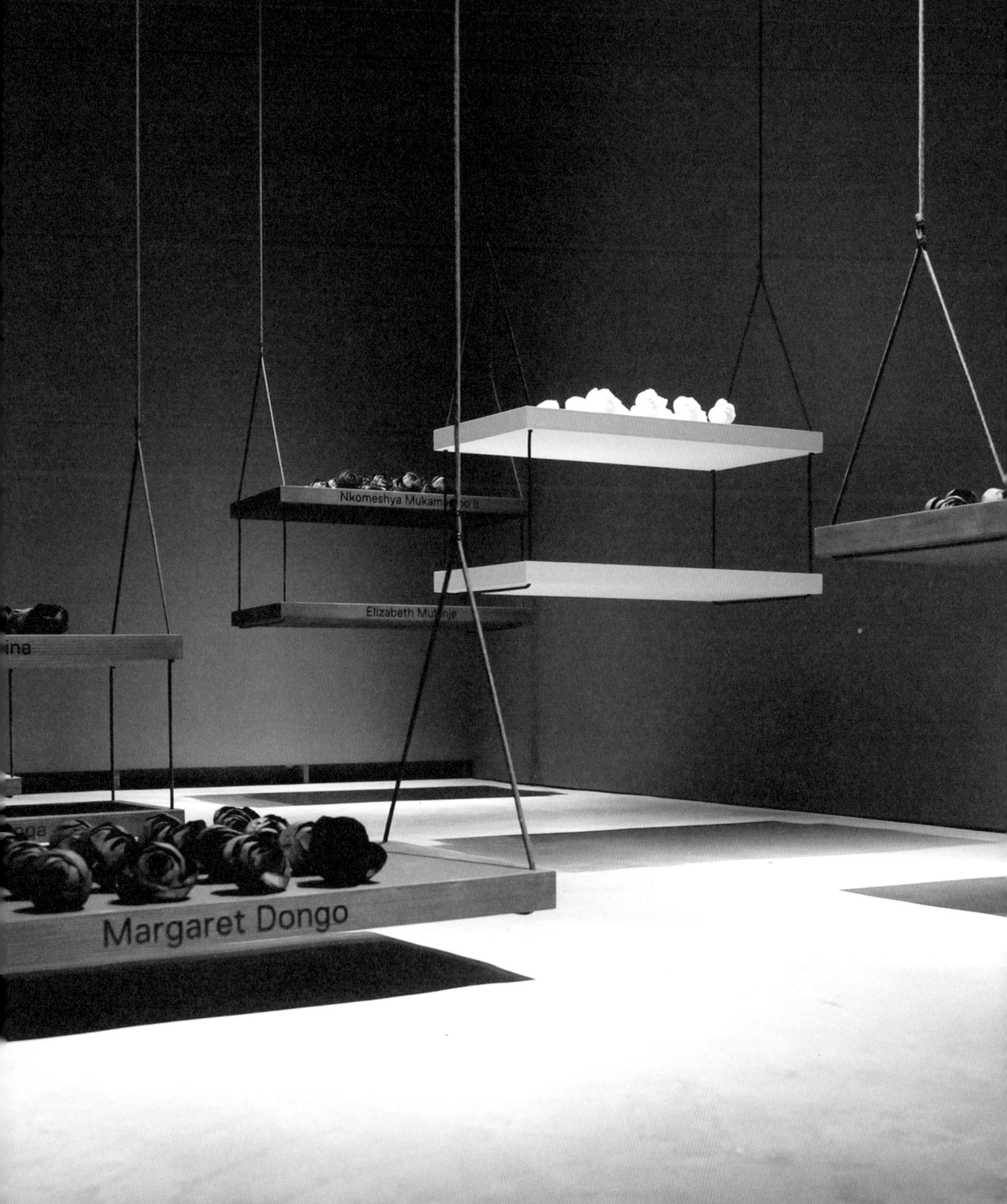
Margaret Dongo

Julia Chikamoneka
Mumba
Chibesakunda

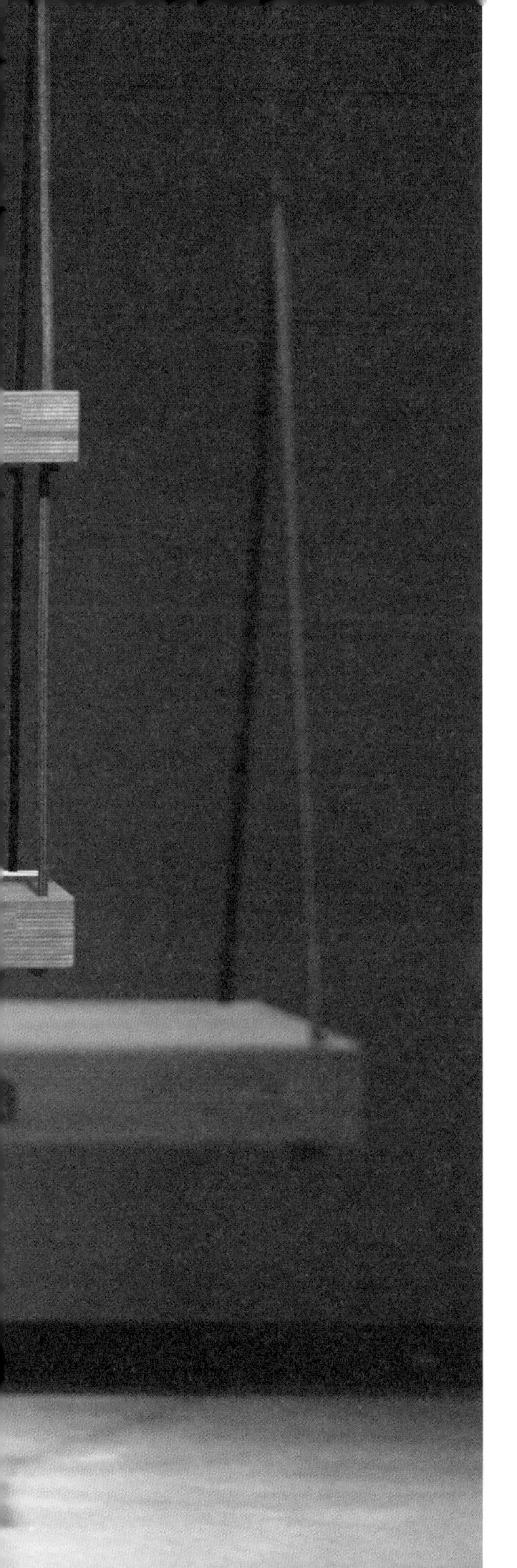

...these wreaths are laid in honour of her memories, 2020

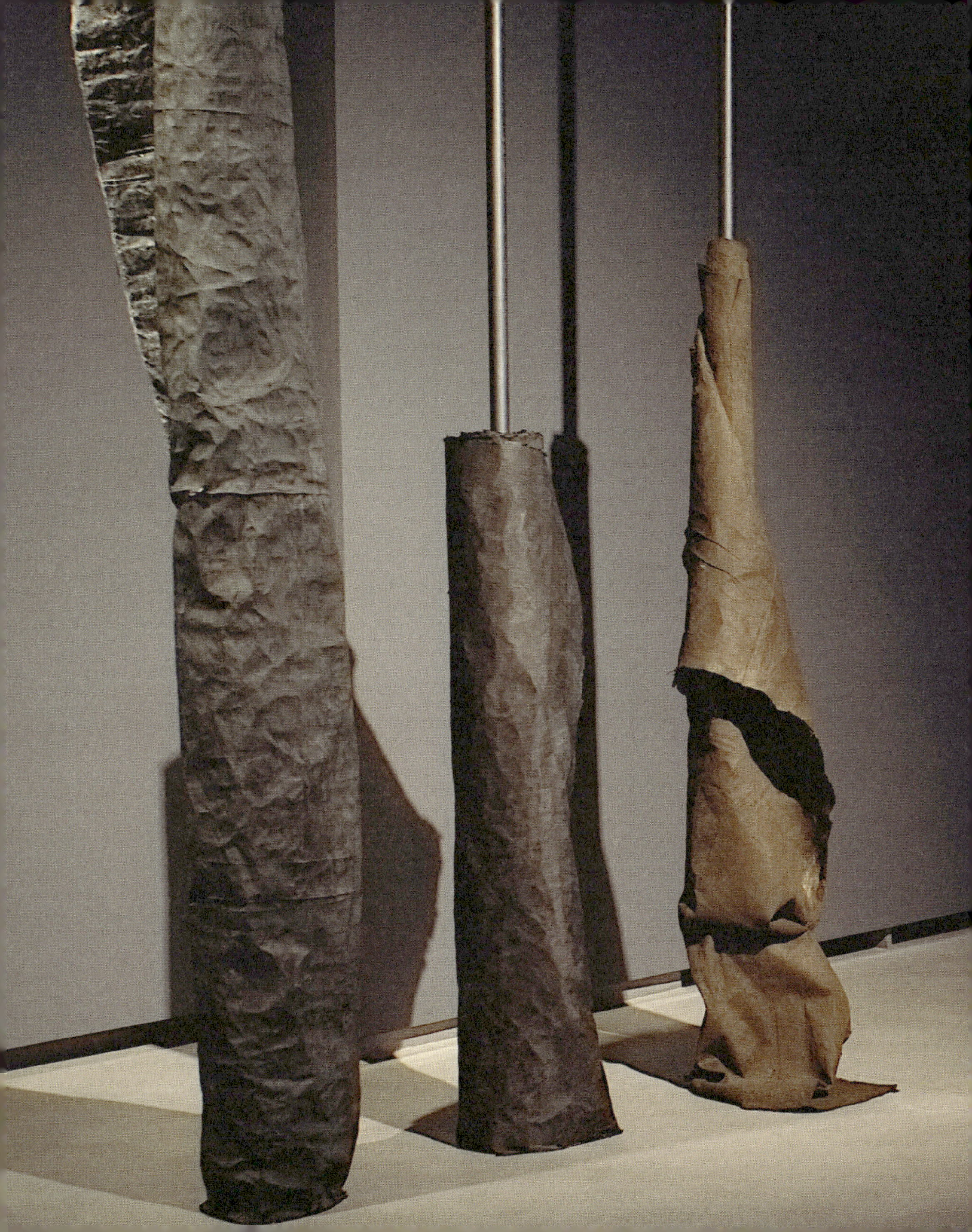

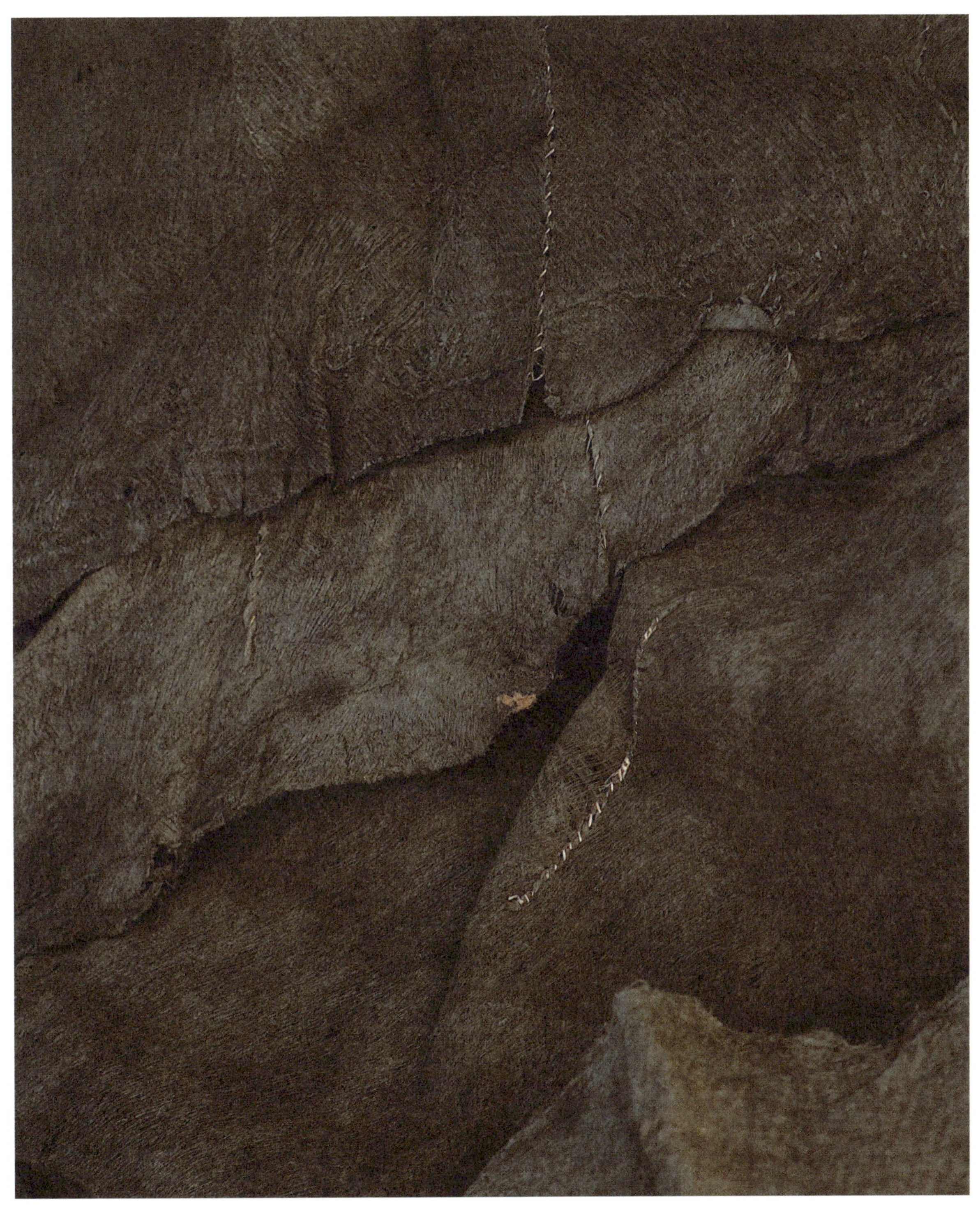

...these moments are spent seeing her invisibility and hearing her silence, 2019–2020

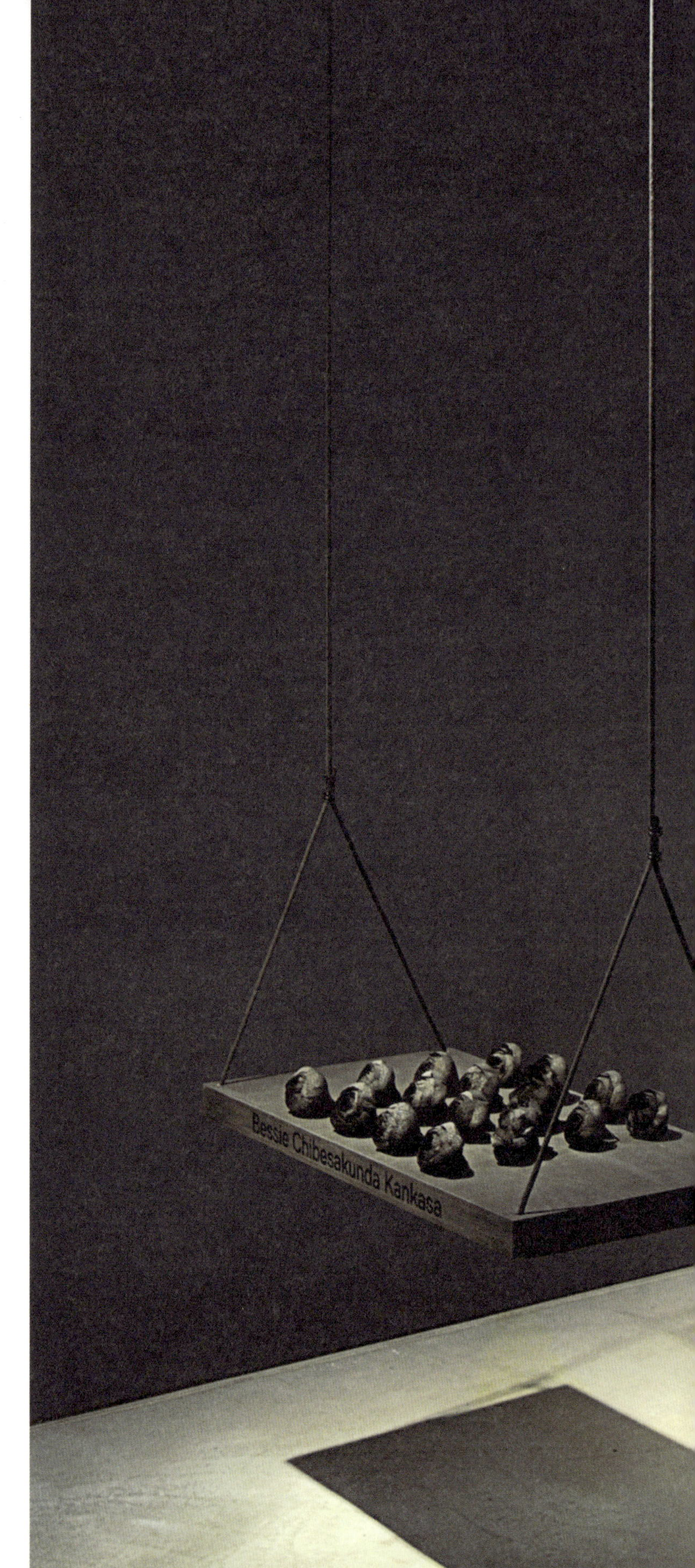

…these wreaths are laid in honour of her memories, 2020

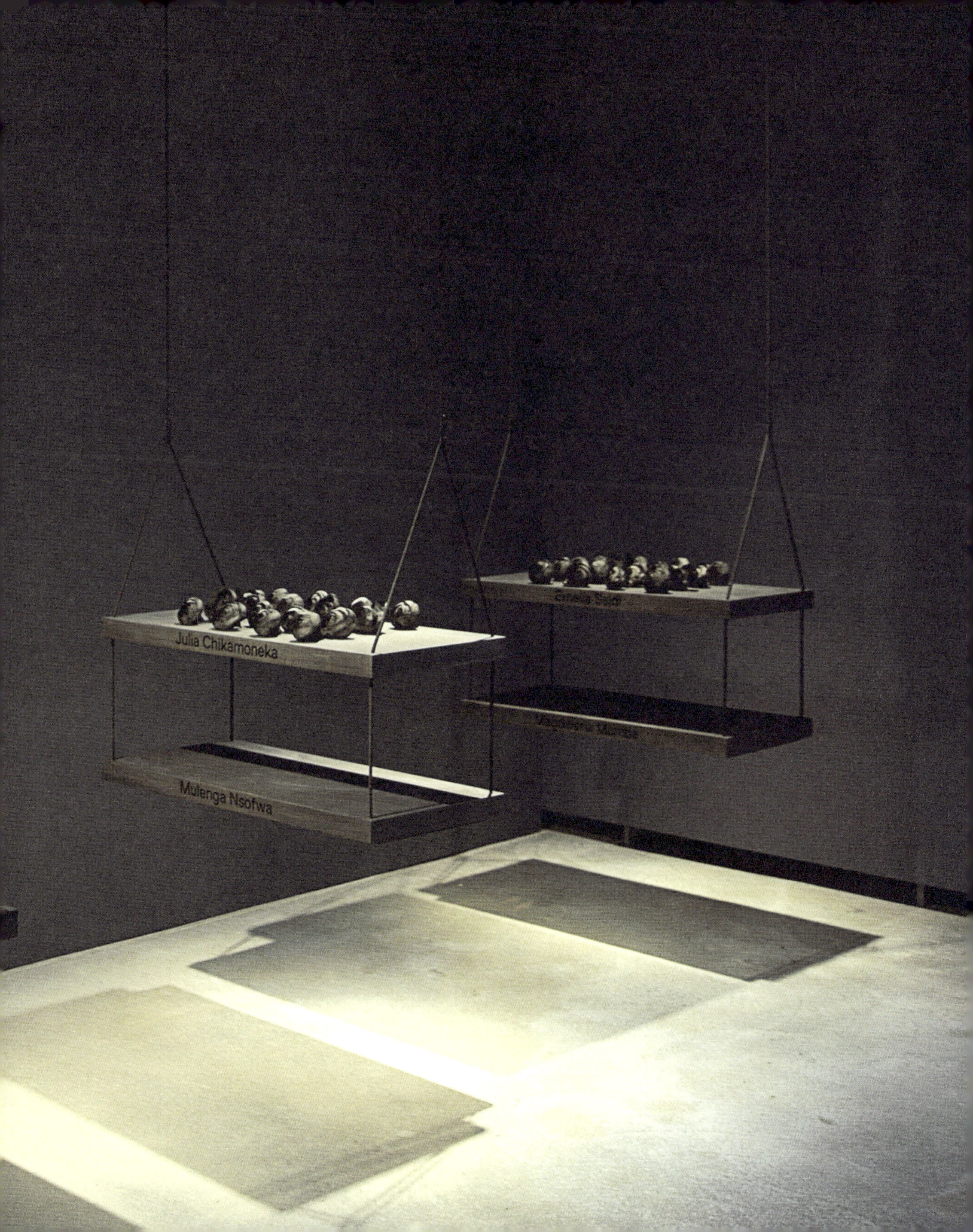
Julia Chikamoneka
Mulenga Nsofwa

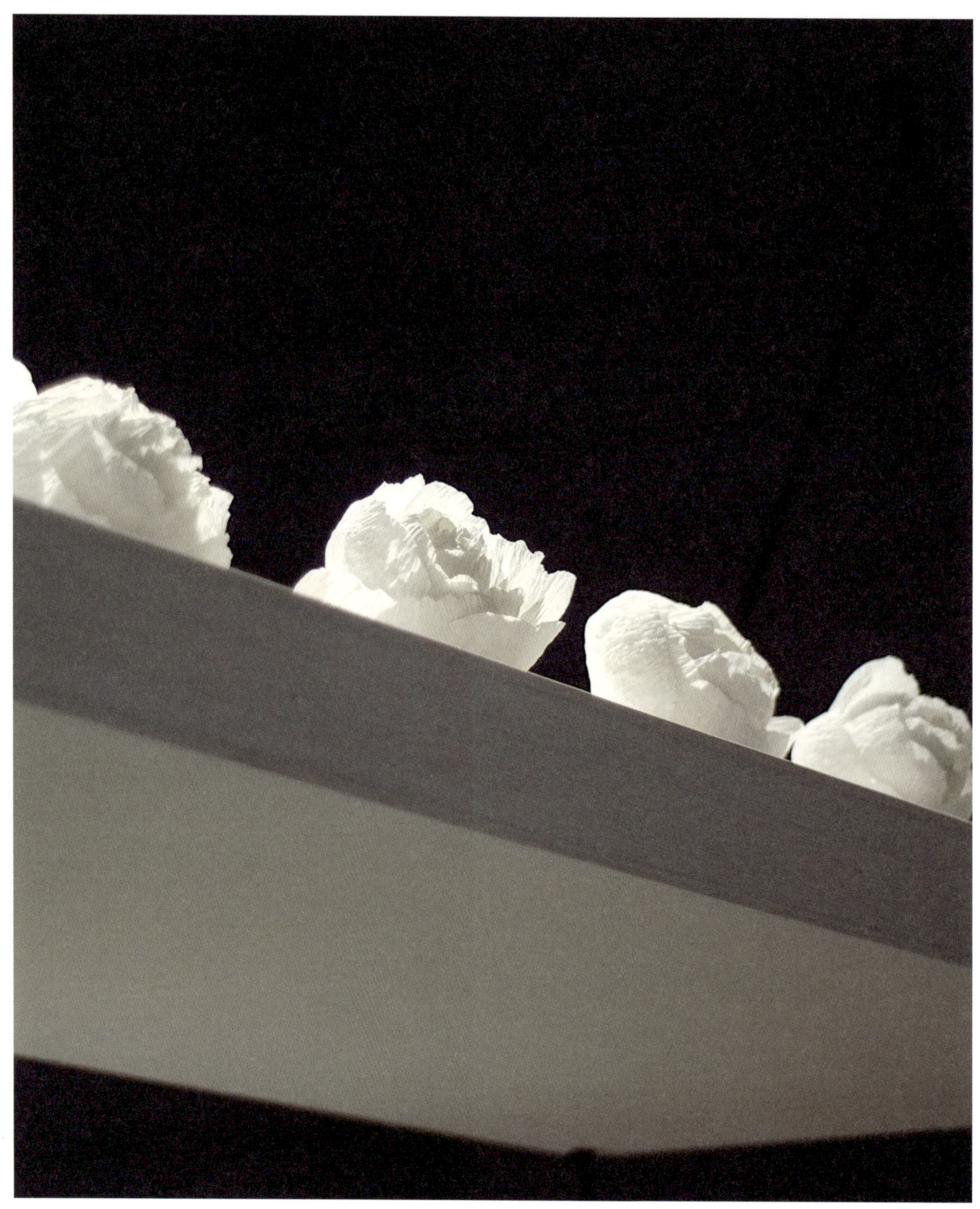

…these wreaths are laid in honour of her memories, 2020

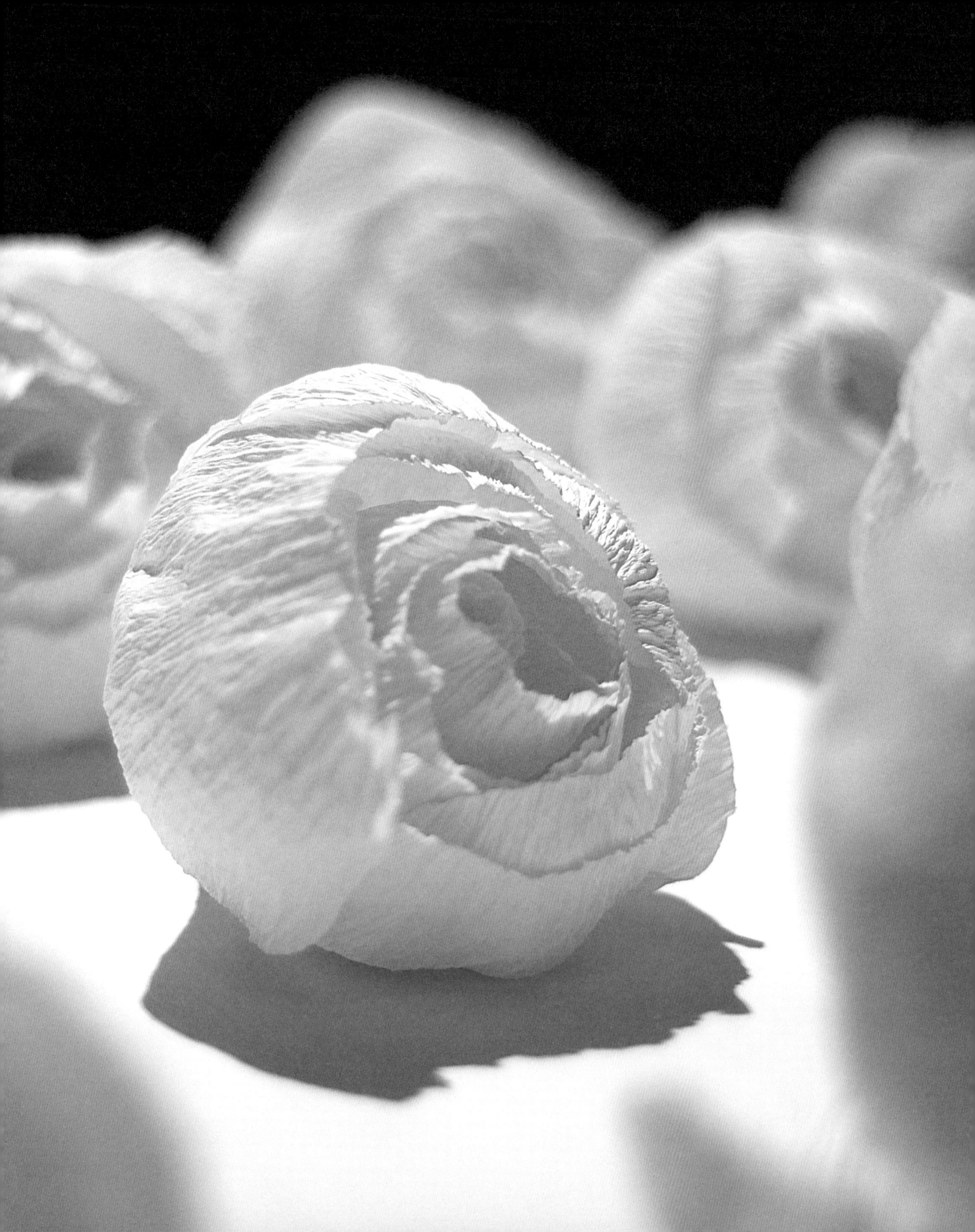

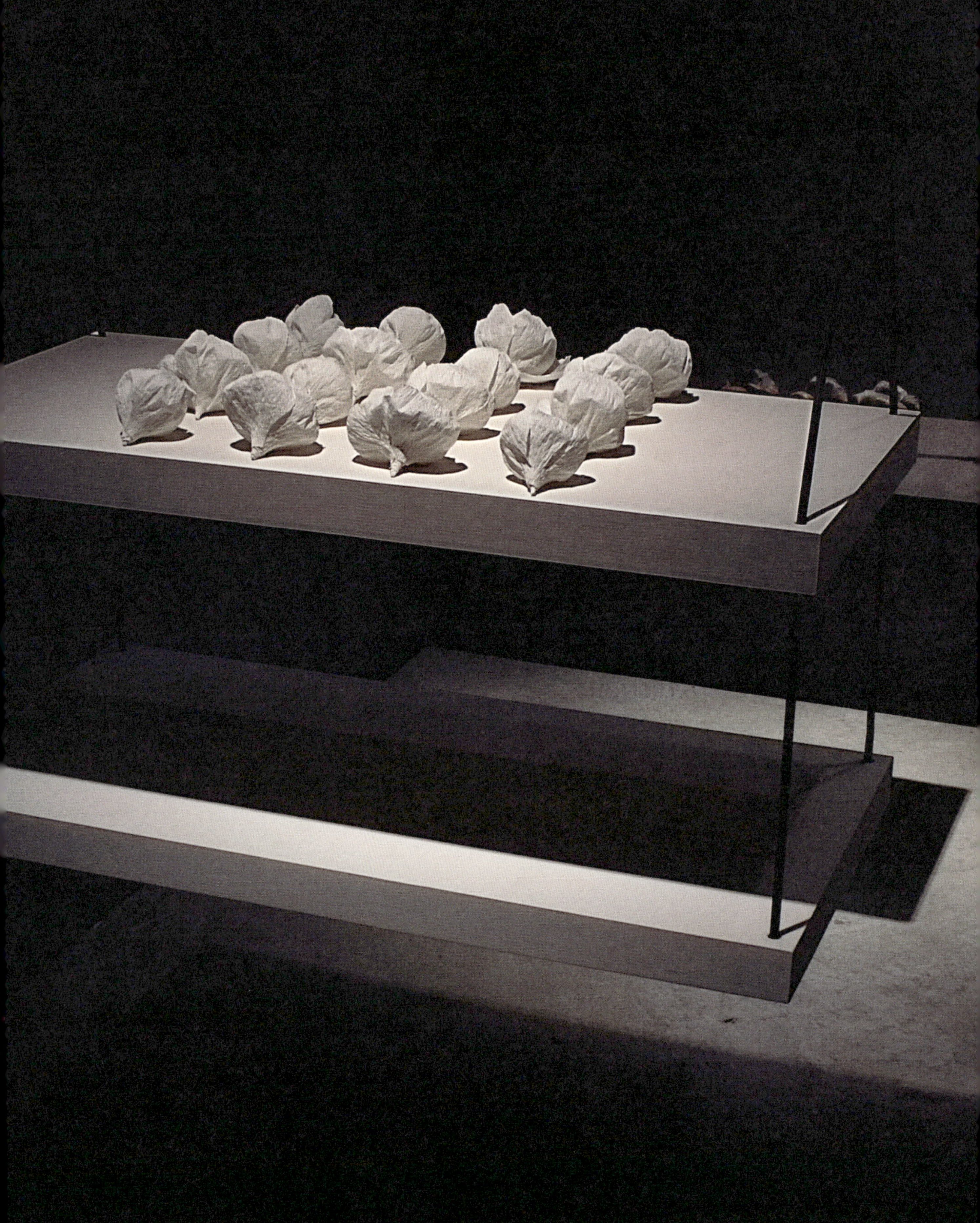

...these wreaths are laid in honour of her memories, 2020

...these practices are done in sharing her stories, 2020

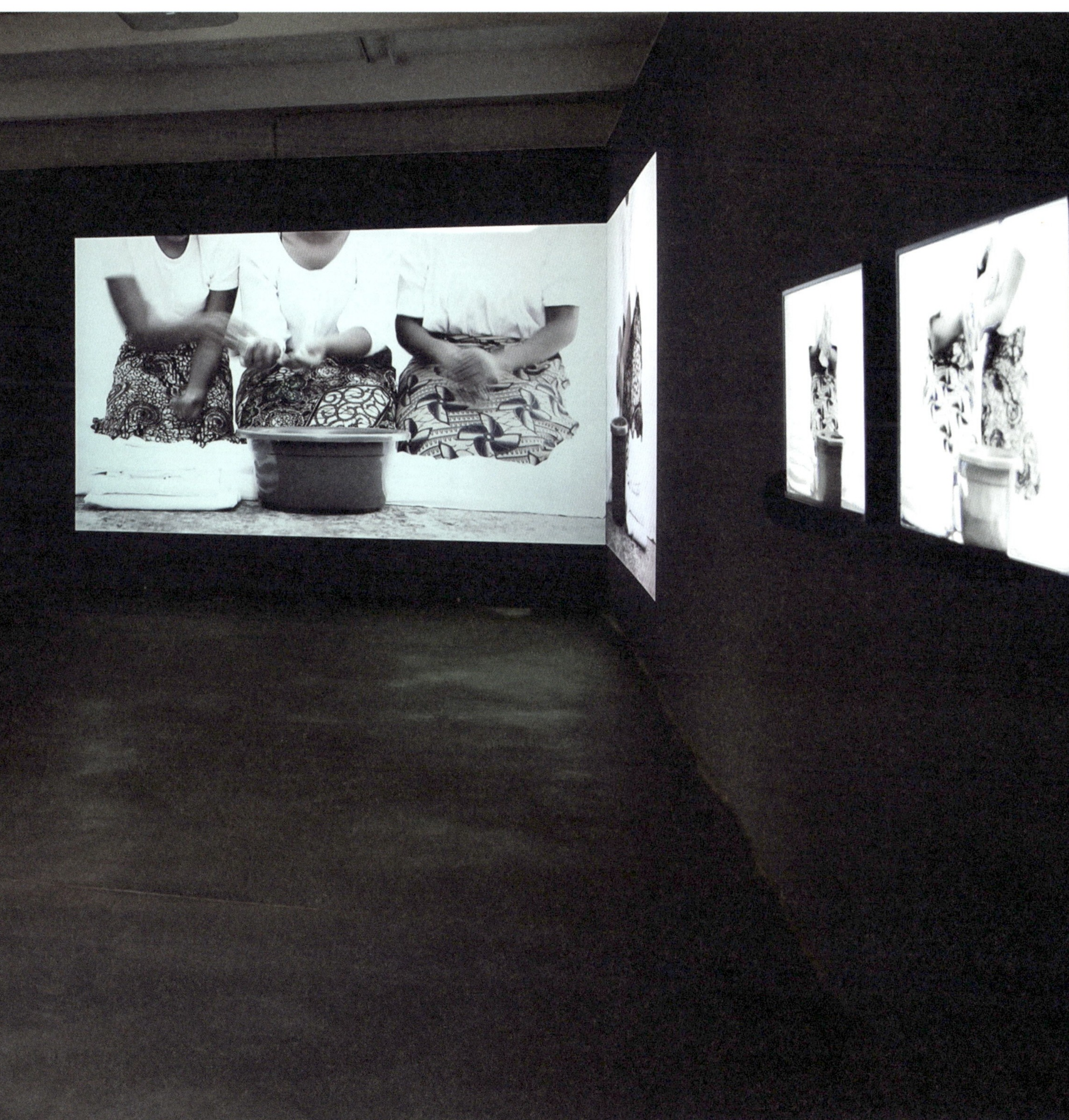

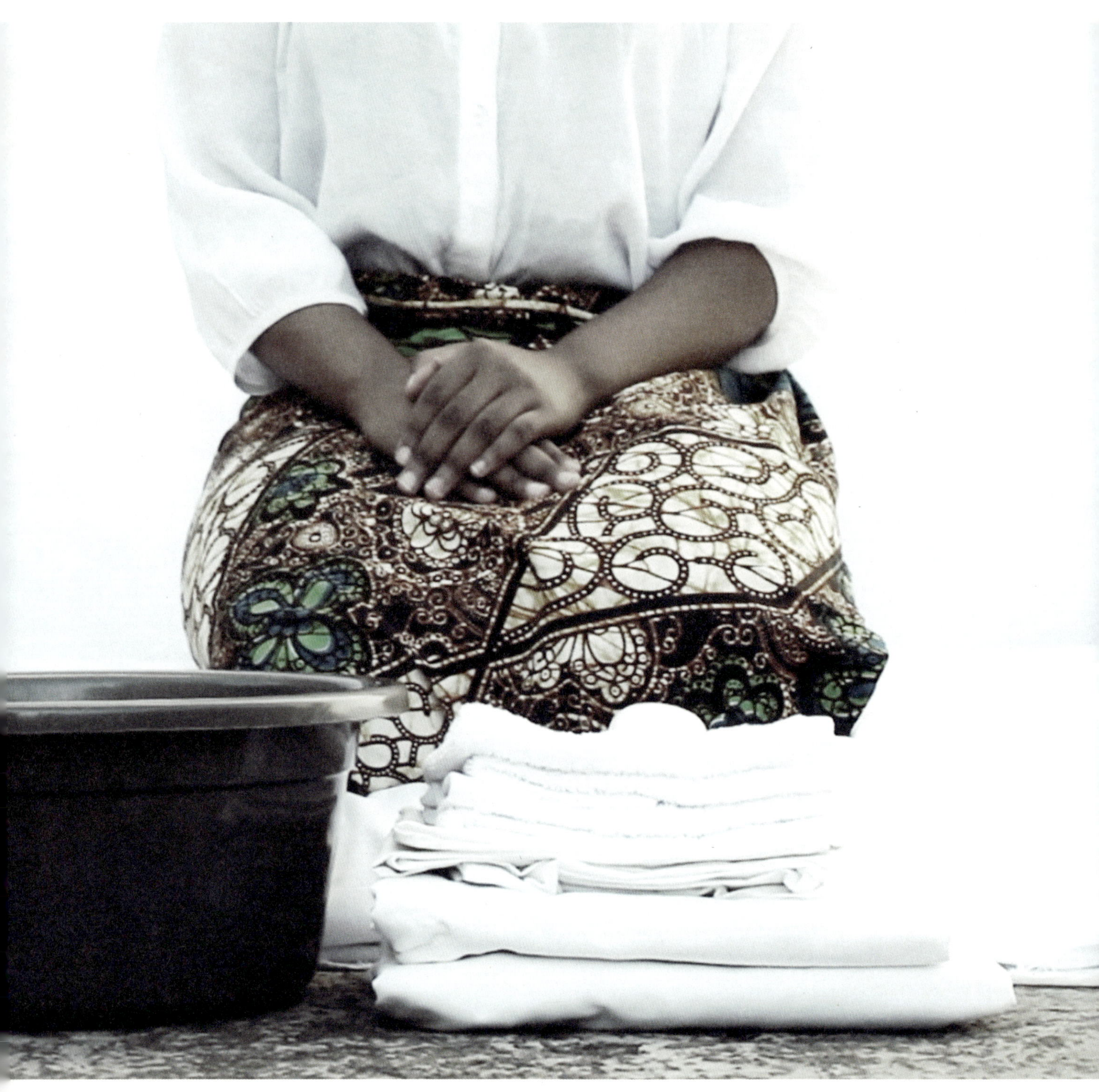

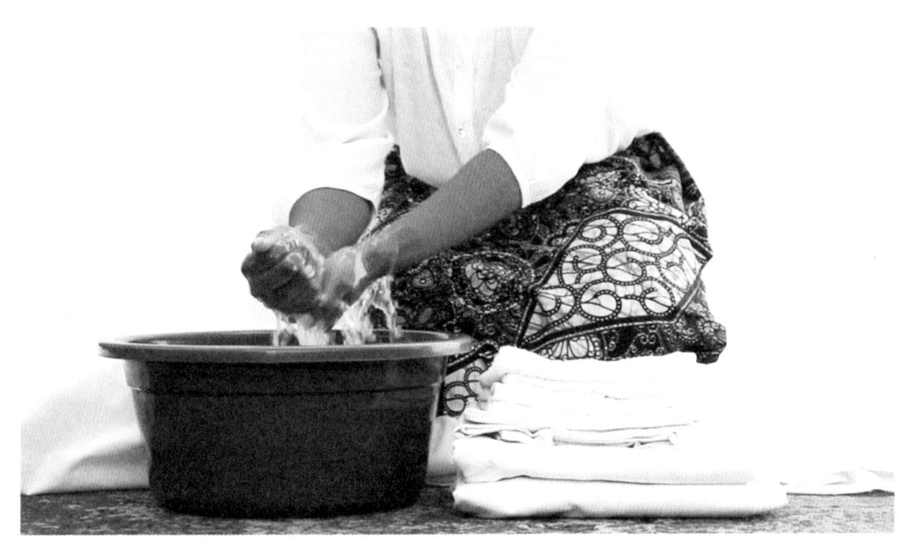

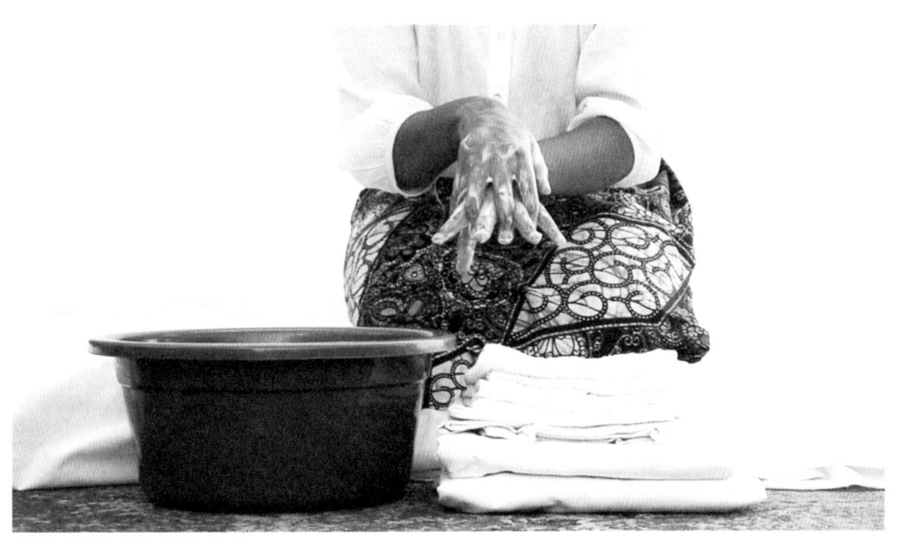

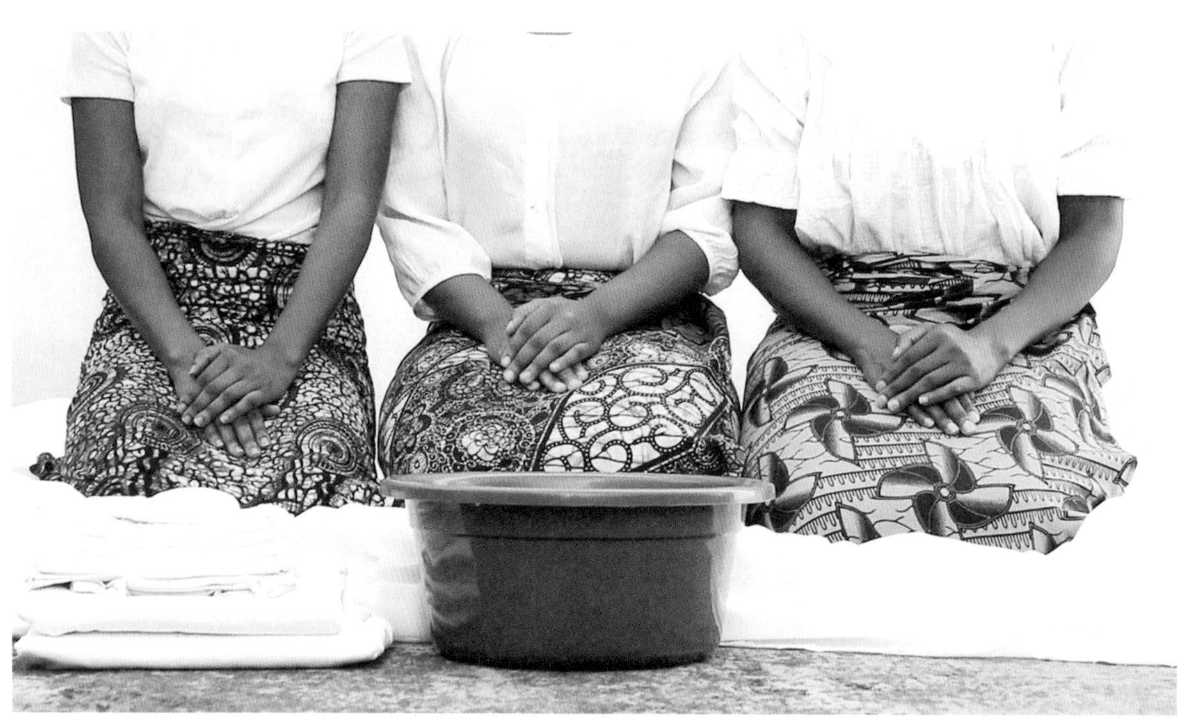

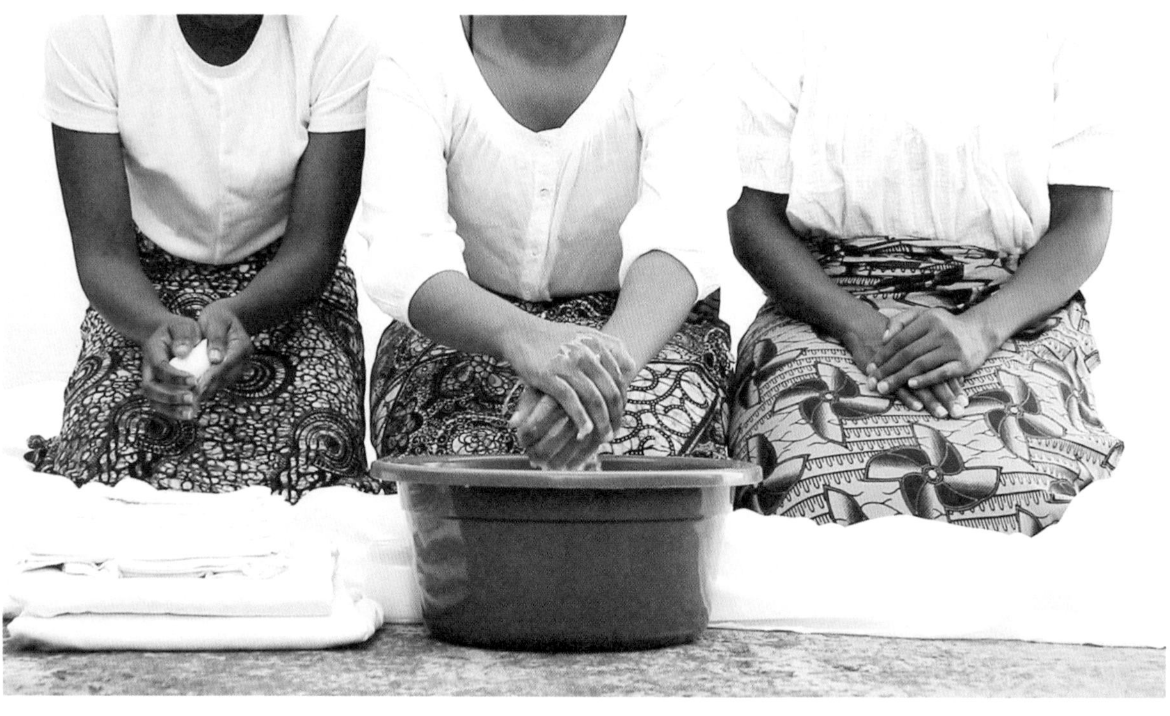

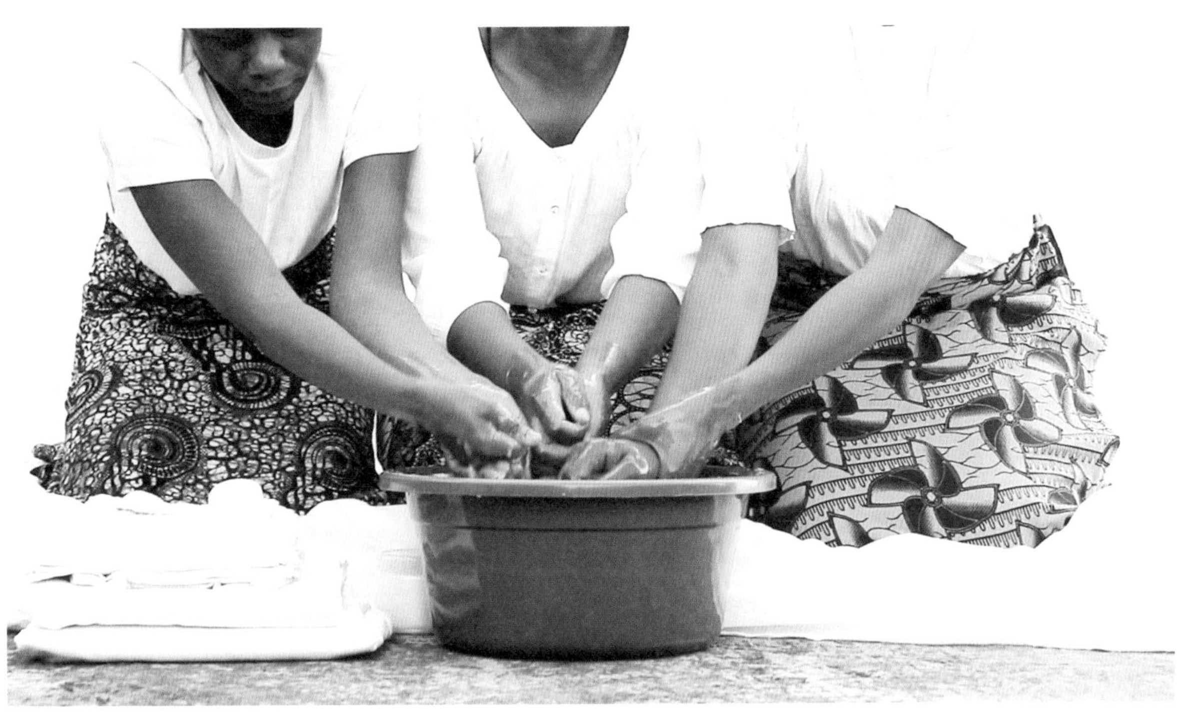

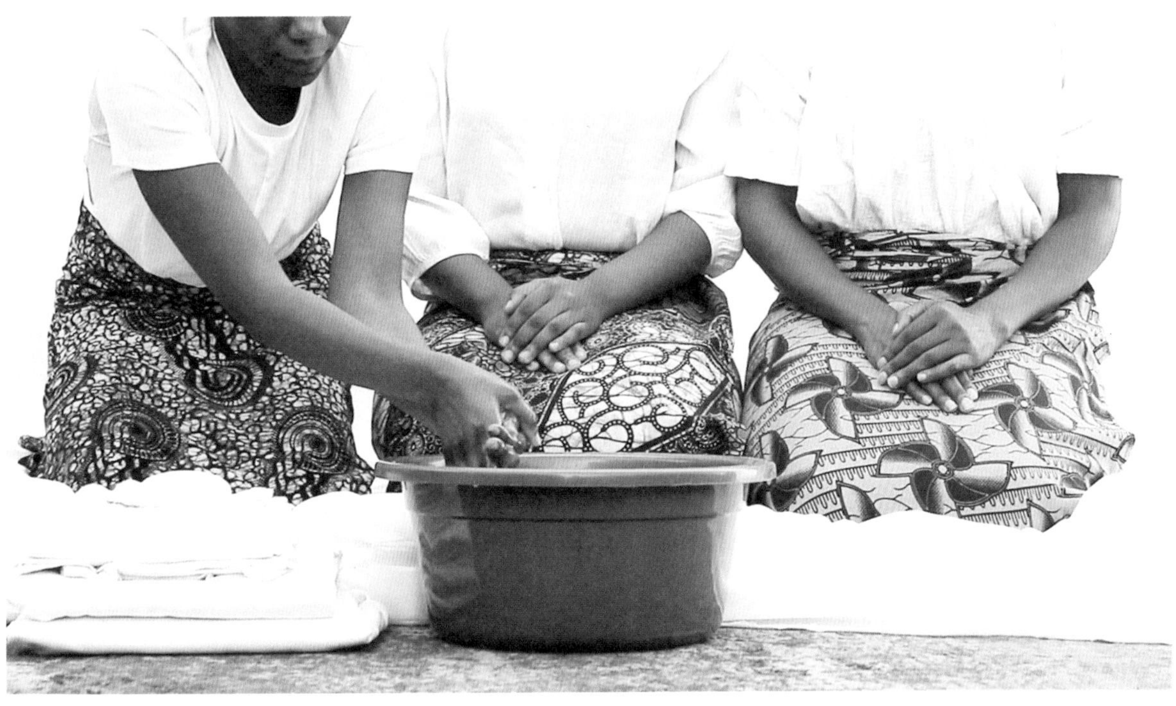

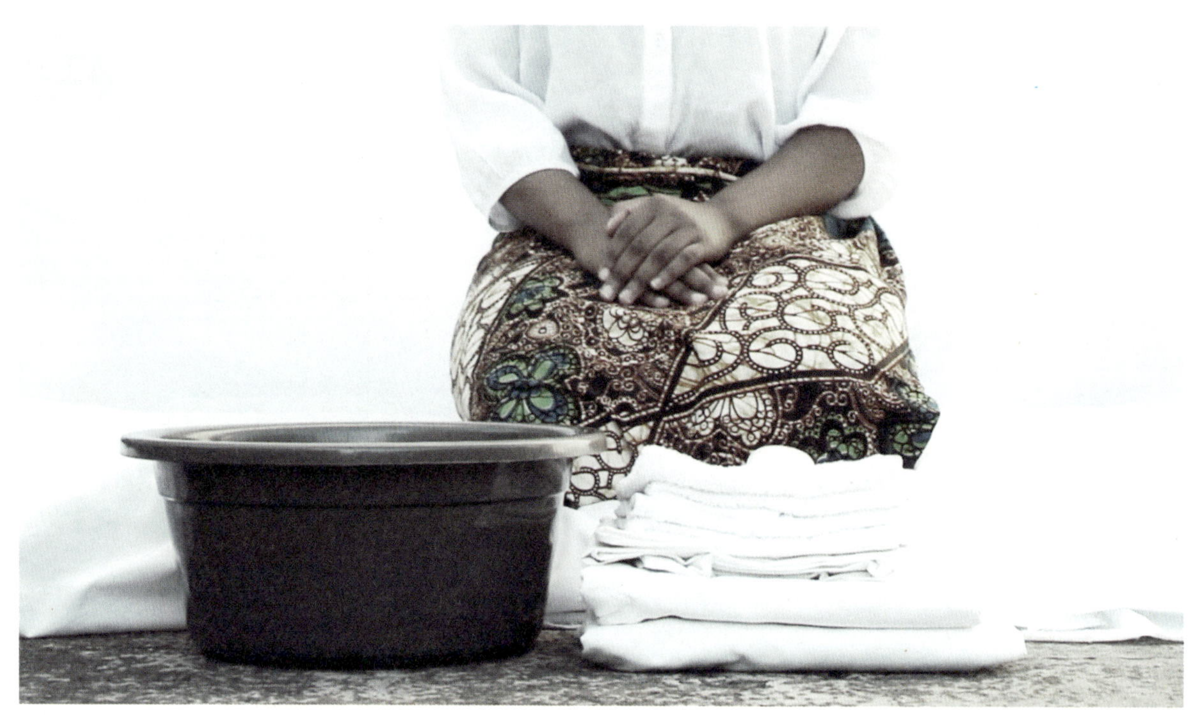

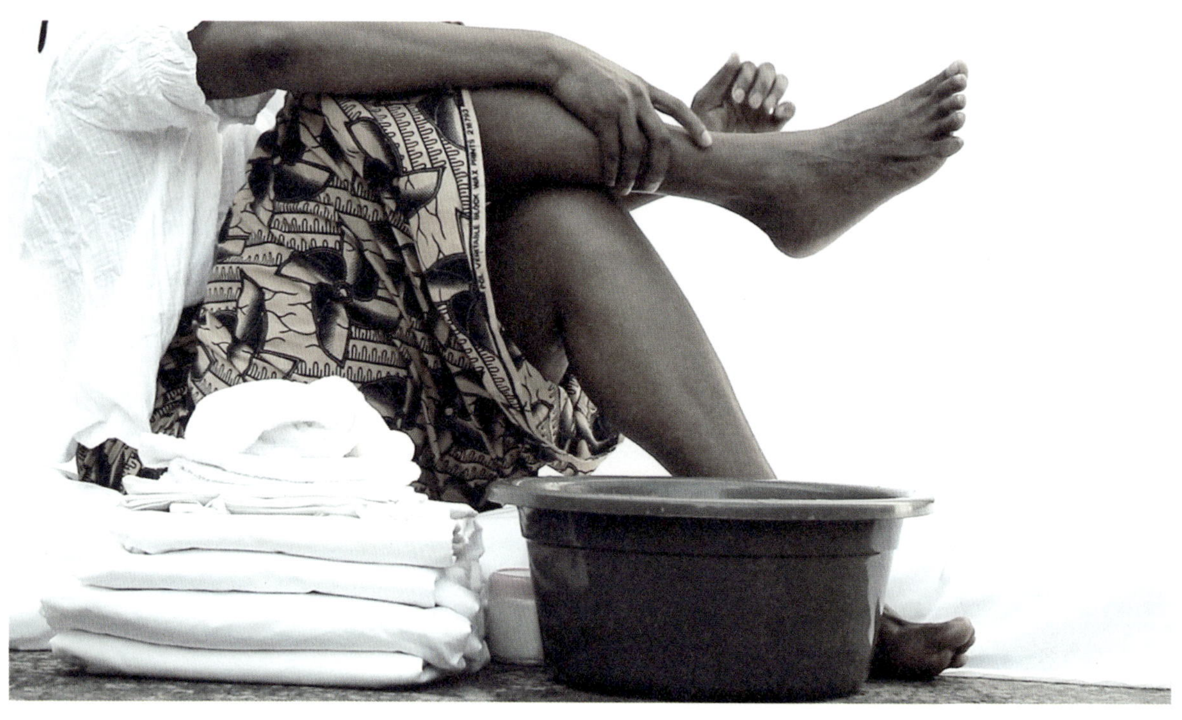

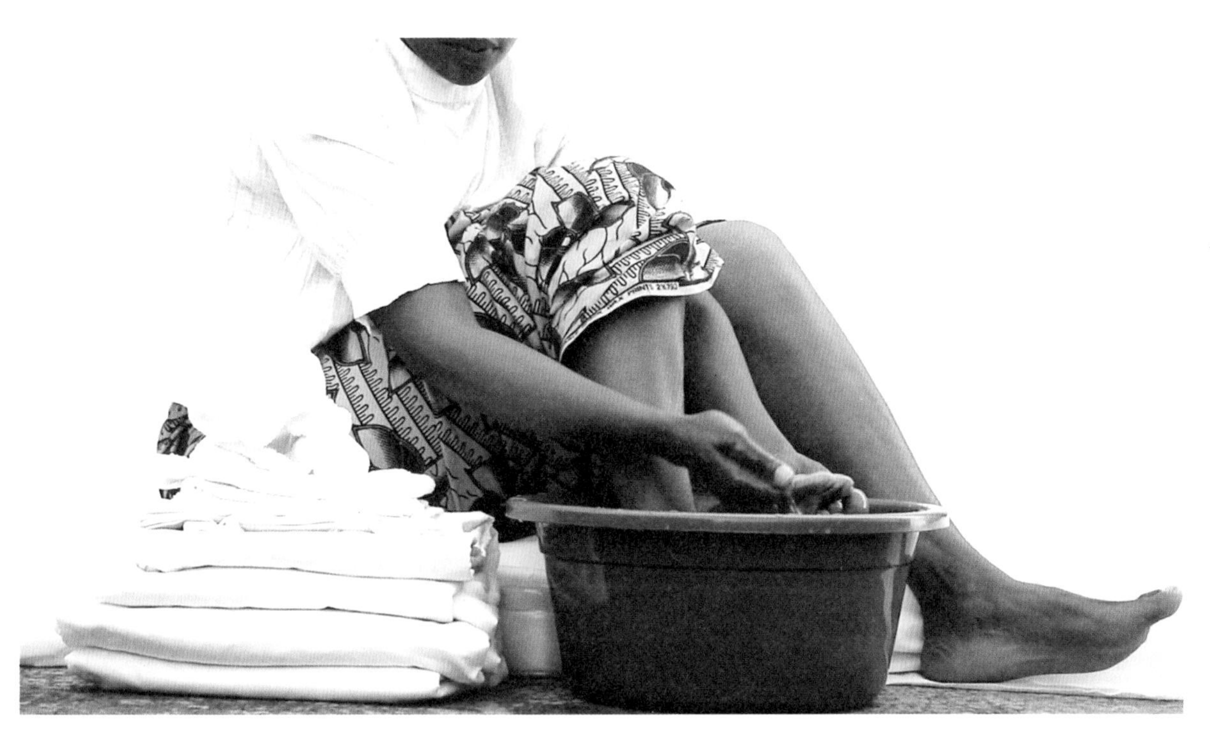

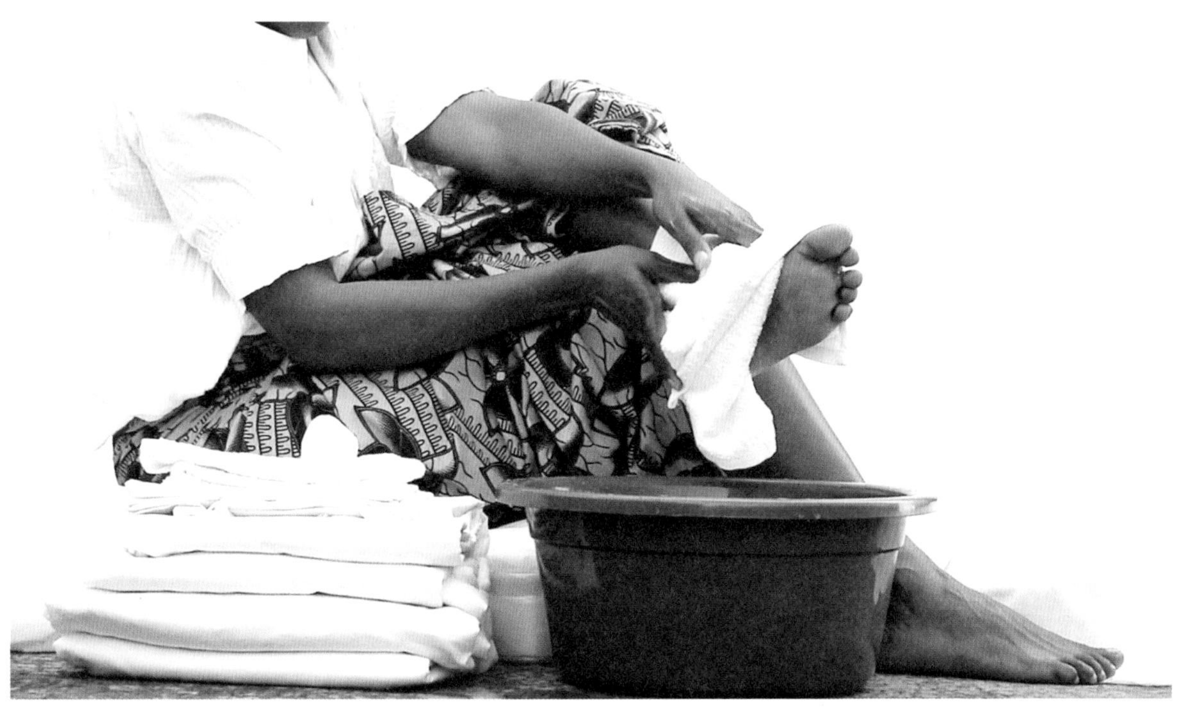

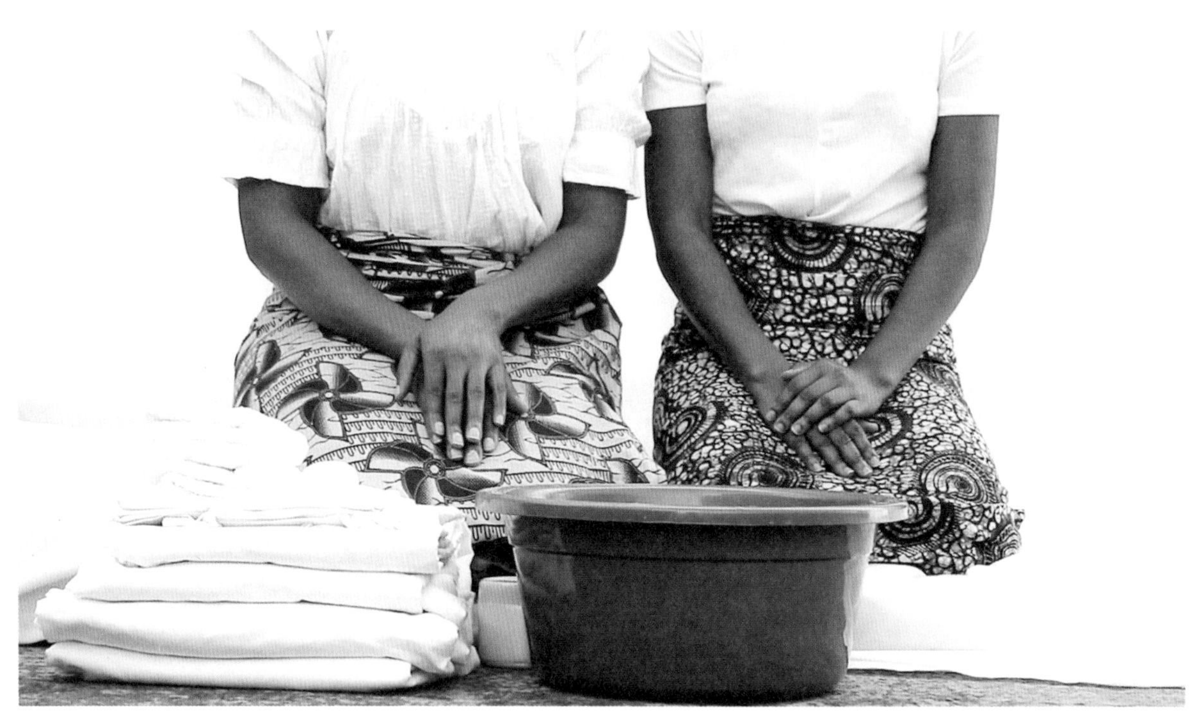

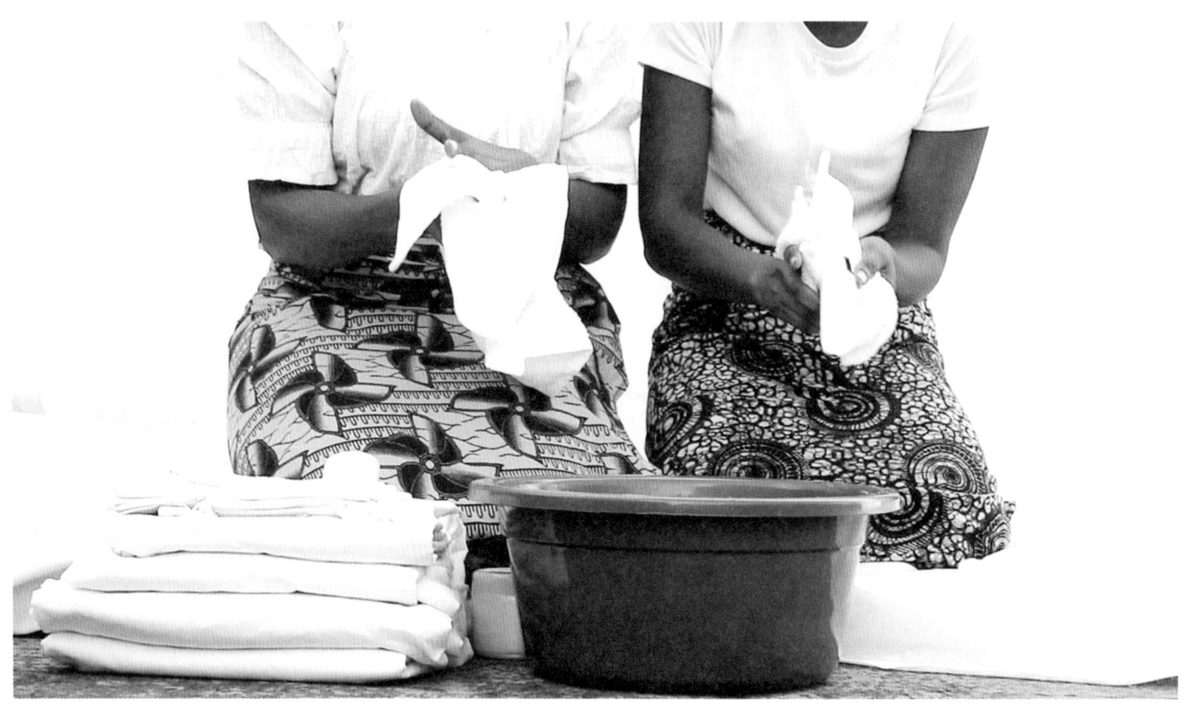

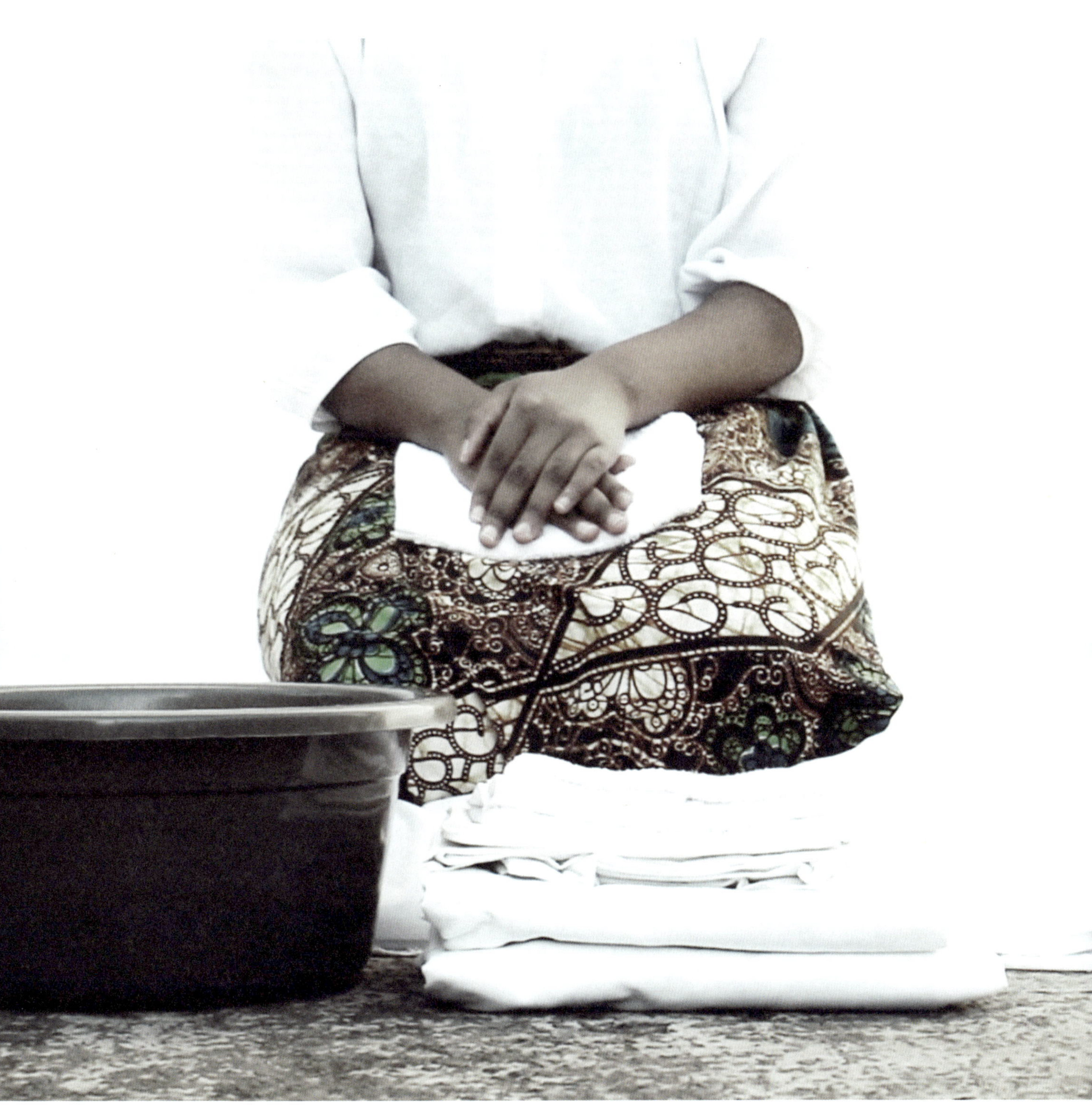

Complexities of Memory

A Conversation between Fadzai Muchemwa and Gladys Kalichini

The following conversation unfolded in the months of March, April and May 2020. At the beginning of the conversation, I was waiting for my study permit for South Africa to be approved and Gladys was at Rhodes University having just begun the third year of her PhD and holding a residency at Künstlerhaus Bethanien in Berlin awarded by KfW Stiftung. Universities suddenly shut down because of the COVID-19 global crisis. Countries closed their borders and went into lockdown which made it impossible to have conversations in person and in specific places. As a result of the worldwide travel restrictions, this conversation developed through messages, voice notes, calls and emails. Against the backdrop of the growing global Corona pandemic, our conversations on research practice, ideology and opinions on art turned into a form of self-therapy in the face of real fears about safety, mental health and community.

Gladys Kalichini's work explores the representation of women in relation to dominant national and colonial histories. She researches the role of female figures within collective memories and investigates how women have been erased from narratives about the struggle for independence in Zambia and Zimbabwe in the 1960s and 1980s. Her artistic practice is based on researching and developing a concept about the (in)visibility of specific female figures within the structures that preserve memories, such as archives, monuments and personal collections in the two southern African countries.

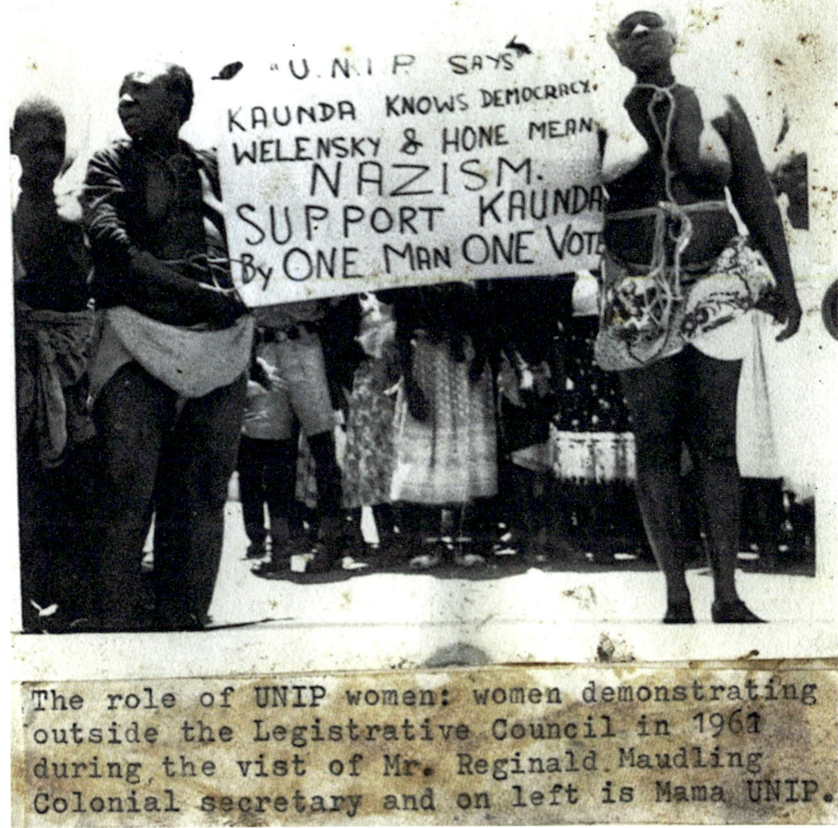

Julia Chikamoneka, Emelia Saidi and Mandalena Mumba during a protest against the constitution proposed by the British for the post-independence state and against the colonial administration, 1961

Fadzai Muchemwa (FM): Can you tell me about your work and how it challenges the dominant national narratives about the past?

Gladys Kalichini (GK): My artistic work draws primarily from stories about national independence and reflects on the representation, the presence or absence of particular women in narrations about history. In a broader context, my work engages with stories about women figures in relation to the telling and remembering of liberation struggles. I am particularly interested in looking at narratives of independence from a multi-layered perspective. I am intrigued by the notion of an archive, both in the physical conventional sense as a site of sanctioned memory and as a retainer which holds traces of memory. My work engages with what I consider the archives' blind spots and some of the ways in which stories about women can be (un)hidden and included within the bigger picture of independence.

FM: How do you navigate different forms of knowledge – photographic, documentary, textual, narrative – about women that you find in archives in Zambia and Zimbabwe?

GK: I think that stories and memories shared from one person to the next, photographs and texts have the power to reveal, and when used as cross references can provide new perspectives on history. I went into archives in Zambia and Zimbabwe initially looking for

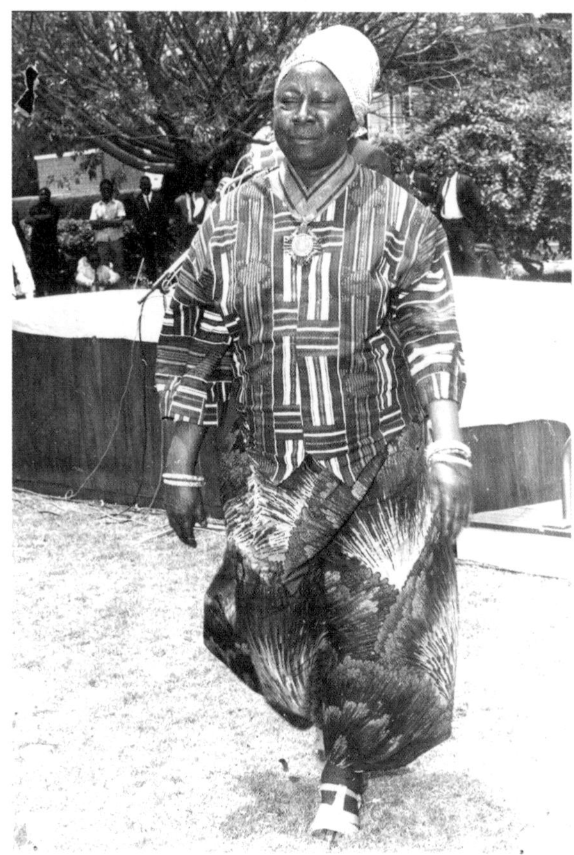

Julia Chikamoneka (1910–1986), undated

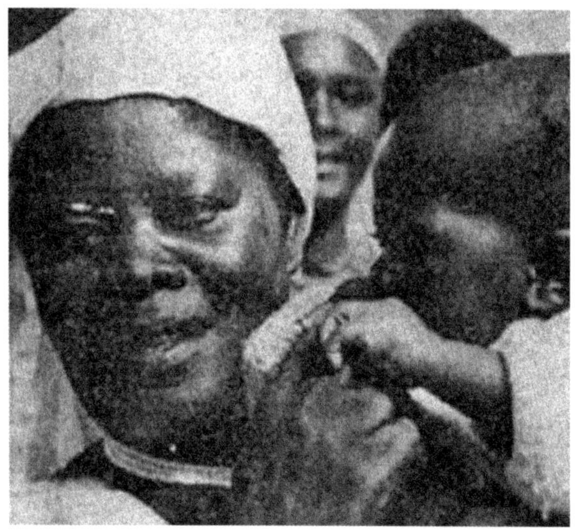

Alice Lenshina (1920–1978), newspaper clipping, 1964

documentation of activities and performances by women. It can be argued that many of these women were involved in the struggle for national independence from British colonial rule. The two countries were formerly known as Northern Rhodesia (Zambia) and Southern Rhodesia (Zimbabwe). While they were liberated at different times, Zambia in 1964 and Zimbabwe in 1980, the activities that unfolded at the cusp of independence are closely linked. Unfortunately, women are hardly ever mentioned in texts, documentary films or traditional primary records about the independence struggles. I then started to look for photographs that were taken in the 1950s and 1960s in Northern Rhodesia, and 1970s and 1980s in Southern Rhodesia. The ones I found became the starting point for making art. For me at that time, the photographs became tangible evidence of traces of women in national histories, they became objects of memory, they somehow became monuments.

FM: What kind of photographs did you find?

GK: I came across one of the most important archival photographs for my work in 2016. The first photograph of women I found inside the archives is an image of Julia Chikamoneka (1910–1986, initially known as Mulenga Nsofwa), Emelia Saidi and Mandalena Mumba that was taken in 1961. This photograph was shot during a protest against a British proposed constitution to be used post-independence and of course against the colonial administration in general. On the picture, the women have undressed and are holding up signs. As I continued to go into the archives in the following years, I found more images, I found pictures of senior Chieftainess Mukamambo Nkomeshya II, Bessie Chibesakunda Kankasa (1936–2018) and I saw clips of newspapers of Alice Lenshina (1920–1978) and of a lot of unidentified and unknown women. In Zimbabwe I heard stories about Amai Musodzi, also known as Elizabeth Maria "Mai" Musodzi Ayema MBE (1885–1952), Joice "Teurai Ropa" Mujuru (b. 1955), Margaret Dongo (b. 1960) and

I also saw photographs of unknown women training in the armed forces to participate in the struggle for independence.

Over time, I have come across documentary films and music which tell the stories of women: among them are *Maudling in Lusaka* (1961)[1] and some liberation songs from Zimbabwe[2]. I also started with interviews and personal conversations with some of these women, in order to supplement the photographs that I found, but also to learn more about the histories that had not been preserved in the archives. I talked to Bessie Chibesakunda Kankasa who is one of the women whose stories my work draws from. She passed away in 2018, but I have video footage and audio recordings. I also was lucky enough to trace Julia Chikamoneka's granddaughter and Mandalena Mumba's great-granddaughter, and a couple of other witnesses. Some of my very elderly relatives like grandmothers and grandaunts were also alive during this period and can recall some events. All these different types of information form archives of knowledge and help me to navigate these stories.

FM: Can you tell me about the work you have done during your residency at Künstlerhaus Bethanien?

GK: My project at Bethanien is titled *… these gestures of memory*. This work is of course an extension of my practice drawing from histories and stories about women. Before I arrived in Berlin, I went to archives and independence monuments in Lusaka (Zambia) and Harare (Zimbabwe). When I arrived in Berlin, I spent time going to monuments and places that have traces of memory such as the Berlin Wall Memorial, the former

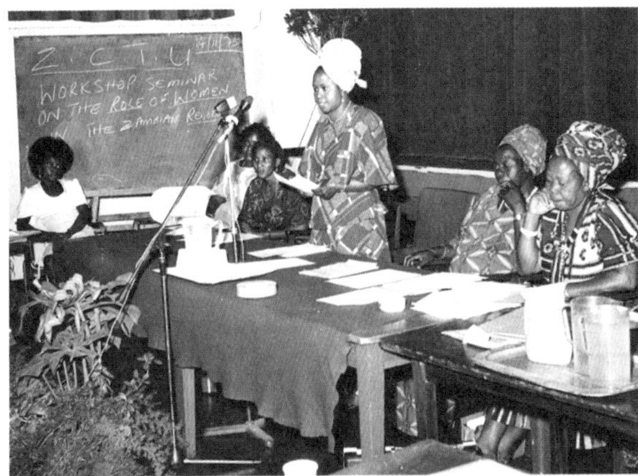

Bessie Chibesakunda Kankasa (1936–2018) speaking at the seminar on the involvement of women in the independence struggle of the Women's Brigade within the United National Independence Party (UNIP), 1975

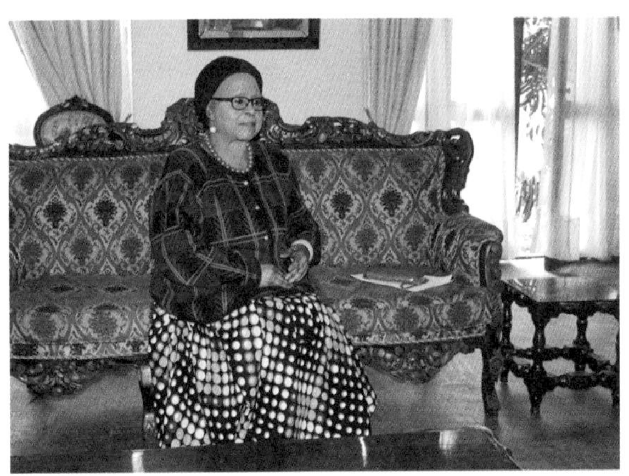

Bessie Chibesakunda Kankasa in 2016 when Gladys Kalichini visited her at home, 2016

1 This short clip shows protests in 1961 in Lusaka, Northern Rhodesia. The protests are against a British proposed constitution to be used in Northern Rhodesia post-independence. British Paté, "Maudling in Lusaka (1961)", 13.04.2020, video, 3:32 min., https://www.youtube.com/watch?v=H4Ar1S-WJws&t=43s.

2 E.g. Zanlaforces1980, "Zanla Forces War Songs", 6.12.2009, video, 7:32 min., https://www.youtube.com/watch?v=0gxerTyYaDs.

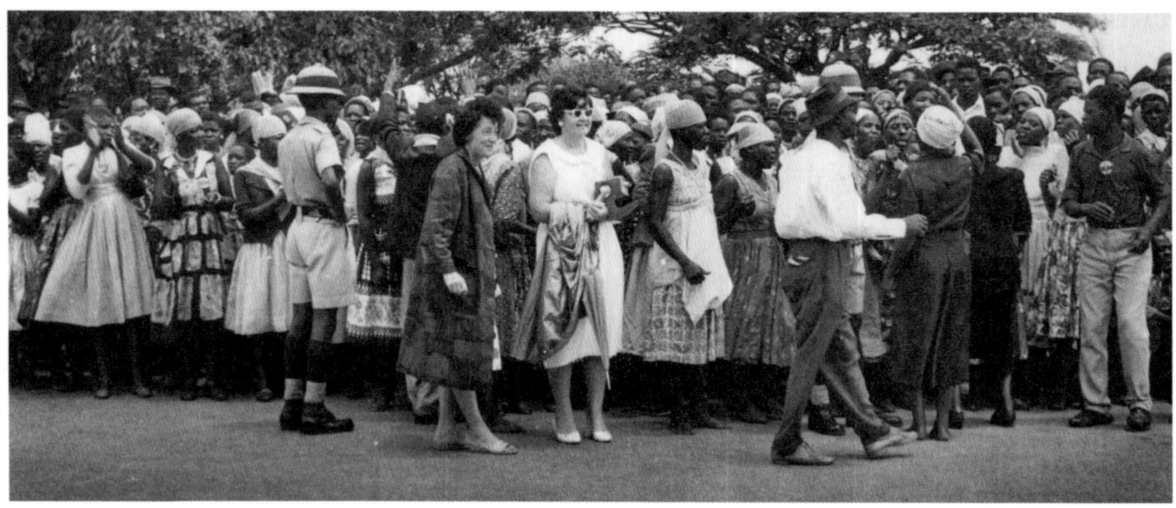

The image shows the UNIP (United National Independence Party) Women's Brigade at a political rally, probably in Lusaka in the 1970s. The woman standing in the centre of the image is Bessie Chibesakunda Kankasa.

East German political prison Hohenschönhausen, the Karl-Marx-Allee which was built by the GDR and the Soviet War Memorial in Treptower Park. These spaces appeared to have the capacity to crystallise memory and make it permanent. My starting point was an idea of performances and gestures of memory, things that we do in an attempt to remember. I am also generally intrigued by practices of mourning, as gestures of commemorating life. In essence, this project is a commemoration for women freedom fighters in Zambia and Zimbabwe and their stories that are somewhat invisible in monumental structures of independence.

In my practice, I conceptualise the process of being overlooked or ignored (erasure/disappearance/becoming invisible) as a process of death. As such, I draw both from the archives and from funerary practices. I am interested in how we attempt to preserve memory and how loss is processed collectively and individually.

FM: *... these gestures of memory,* how are these gestures of memory tied to the recalling of forgotten and hidden stories, and how does it connect to your previous work?

GK: In my previous project titled *Chamoneka: UnCasting Shadows* (2017) and *Fyamoneka: Exploring the Erasure of Women Within Zambian History* (2017), I focused largely on narratives about specific women as the memory and as a body in the process of death. I considered archives as complex spaces were an actual memory could be buried like at a graveyard, or could be stored and observed as if in a mortuary or a place where the story could itself protest erasure. This project at Künstlerhaus Bethanien incorporates more than just the memory but expands to consider the gestures performed around loss and commemorating by viewers and mourners. I also move outside of the archives and consider the notion of a monument as a space of memory.

FM: It's interesting that in your new work you talk about creating monuments. When I think of monuments, I think of them as being created not lest we forget but more like lest we remember. I feel that monuments reinforce dominant narratives.

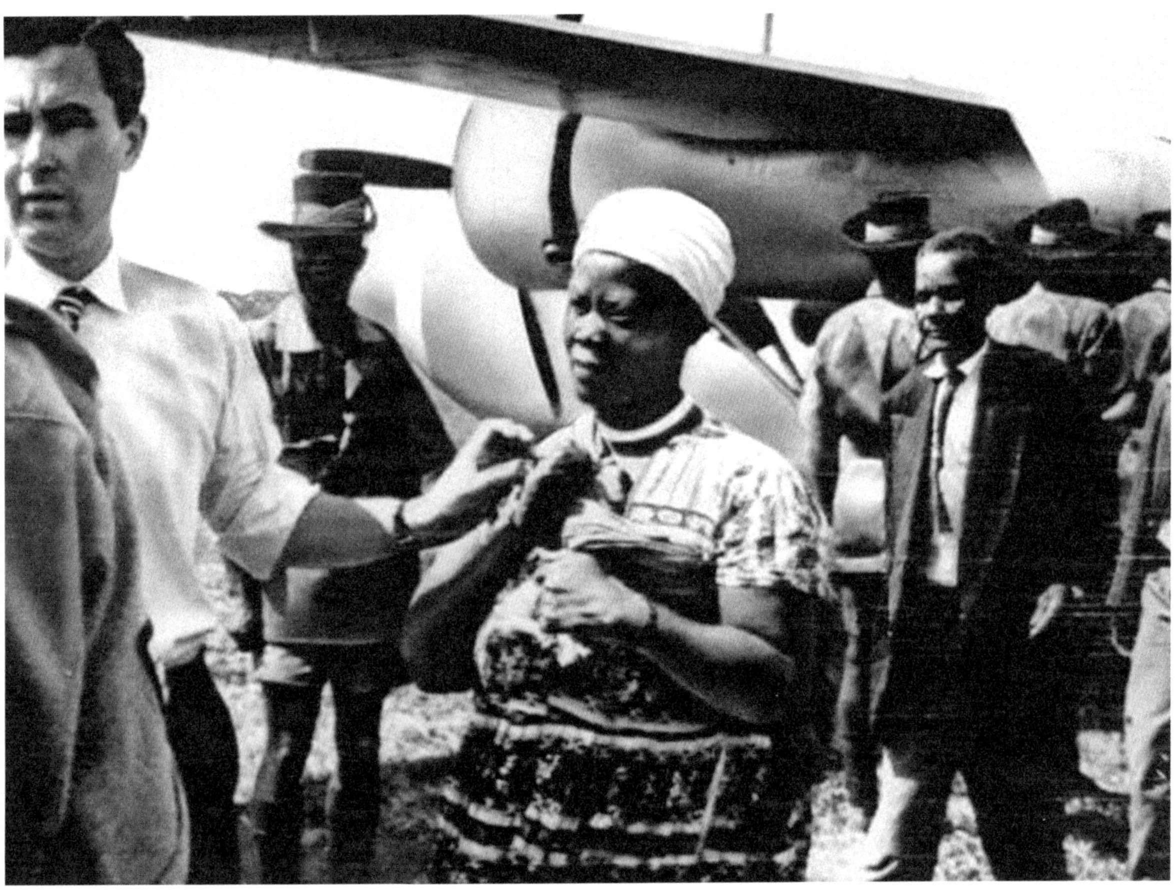

Alice Lenshina, newspaper clipping, undated

GK: In part I agree with you, that in some ways national monuments do reinforce particular narratives. However, here I am reminded of Pierre Nora's (1989)[3] concept of memorial places, that particular places are retainers of memory, but memory in itself is complex. He argues that memory is constantly evolving – and is open to the dialectics of remembering and forgetting. I think of monuments in this way too: even though at times they reinforce particular dominant memories, at the same time they are spaces where memory is constantly in flux. On one end, my work attempts to create memorial spaces for particular women, and, on the other, one can perceive the work as being counter-monumental, in that it does highlight and acknowledge a gap within the dominant narrative. They are monuments that subvert and challenge the bias that is inherent in dominant narratives.

FM: When I met you in 2016, you were working on ideas about erasure, death and Julia Chikamoneka's and Alice Lenshina's political narratives. Our conversation then

3 Pierre Nora, "Between Memory and History: Les Lieux De Mémoire", in *Representations*, no. 26, special issue: *Memory and Counter-Memory* (Spring 1989), pp. 7–24. Accessed June 8, 2020, doi:10.2307/2928520.

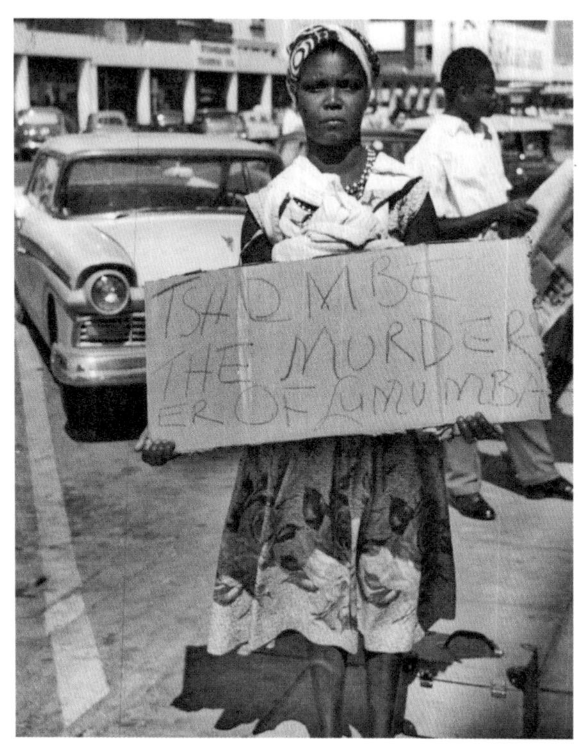

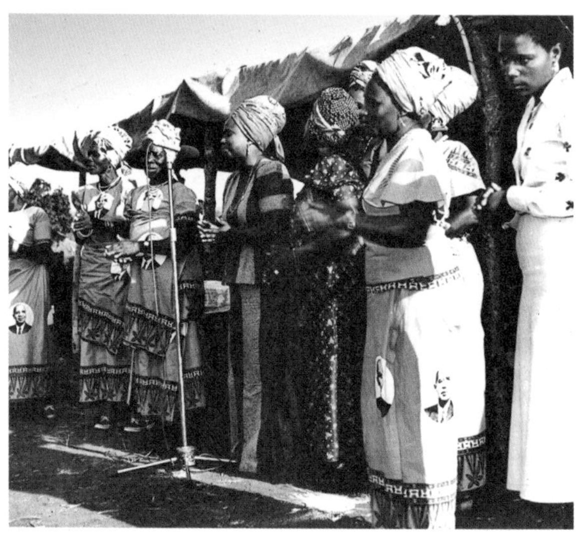

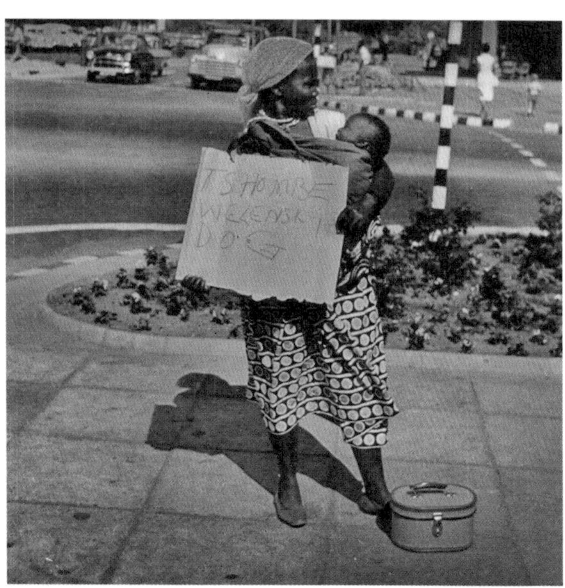

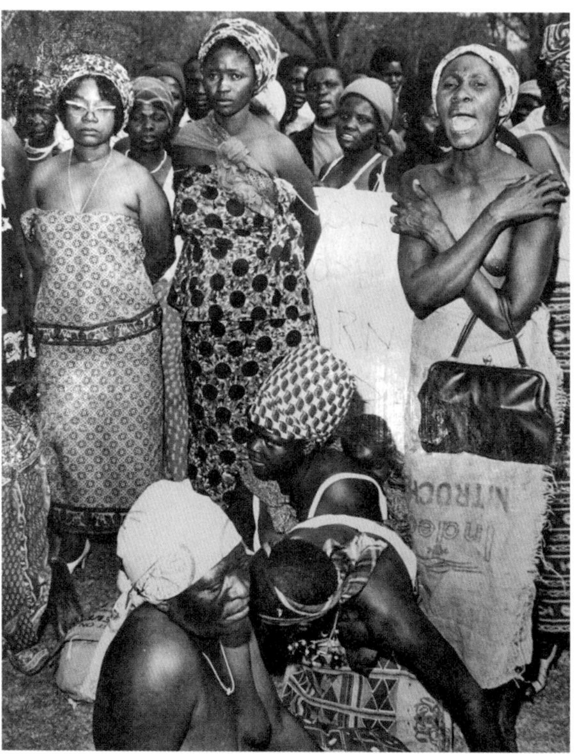

Unnamed women participating in the struggle for independence in Zambia, dates unknown

focused on erasure as removal, blind ways of seeing and misrepresentations. In *Burial: Erasing Erasure* (2017) you explored burial processes in relation to the removal and hiding of bodies. What is your view of burial and embodiment in relation to the archive and black female bodies?

GK: The work you allude to here is part of the body of work in *Chamoneka: UnCasting Shadows*. In this work, I used death as a metaphor for the process of erasure and bodies to reference stories or memories of women. I was looking at the process of burying bodies and exhuming them and then presented it as a protest against erasure. In the specific video and voile cloth installation you mention, I staged a practice from some Zambian cultures: when a deceased one is being buried, certain mourners are covered in a white powder. After the body is buried, a tombstone is placed above the grave and at a later time unveiled and a memorial service is had. For me this performance relates really to the hiding of the body by burying it, and consequently ensuring that the deceased is not forgotten through the gestures that are performed later on, such as the memorial service.

FM: From your previous response it appears as though you incorporate your personal experiences of loss into your method of dealing with missing narratives in archival collections.

GK: Absolutely true. I draw from personal experiences and practices that unfold within my context in order to understand how loss and death is dealt with. My way of making art can also be thought of as making mourning spaces and understanding what it means, psychologically and physically, to try to commemorate something that is no longer visible or present. I think dealing with loss and mourning can be linked to memorialising. It is important that I acknowledge that while mourning can differ from one society to the other, that it is something that is common to all. When creating my work, I submerge myself to understand the archival research and connect that to the experiences of my society, culture and history.

FM: In *... these gestures of memory*, do you draw from any mourning practices from Zambia or Zimbabwe?

GK: For this project, I collaborated with some of my female relatives and friends in some works. When the borders were closed, I had to rethink the form of some of the work, I designed a video installation comprising four synchronised videos. Some of the videos show clips of three of my friends, one Ugandan and two South Africans wearing *ifitenge* that my mother gave to me and I have worn to different funerals. This work looks at ideas of cleansing during mourning, washing of bodies, ideas about women sharing stories and experiences of other women, and the blurring of lines between individual and collective mourning. It explores ideas of collective caring, and not just amongst women but also across a cultural spectrum.

FM: It is fascinating to hear about the evolution of your work. You incorporate ideas about community caring which is highly relevant today, especially considering the situation that the world is in right now. There is of course the Covid-19 pandemic and an uprising calling for the recognition and betterment of black lives across the world. Your work evokes a need to recognise and to remember the stories of women who have participated in the liberation of Zambia and Zimbabwe and to an extent of many other nations. I am curious to know what the other works in your exhibition are like and how they relate to the video installation made in collaboration with your family and friends.

GK: Before I even talk about the other work, I would like to mention that when I started on this exhibition, the borders were open and mobility was really not an issue for me, and of course I had thought of my work manifesting in a particular way. But in the situation

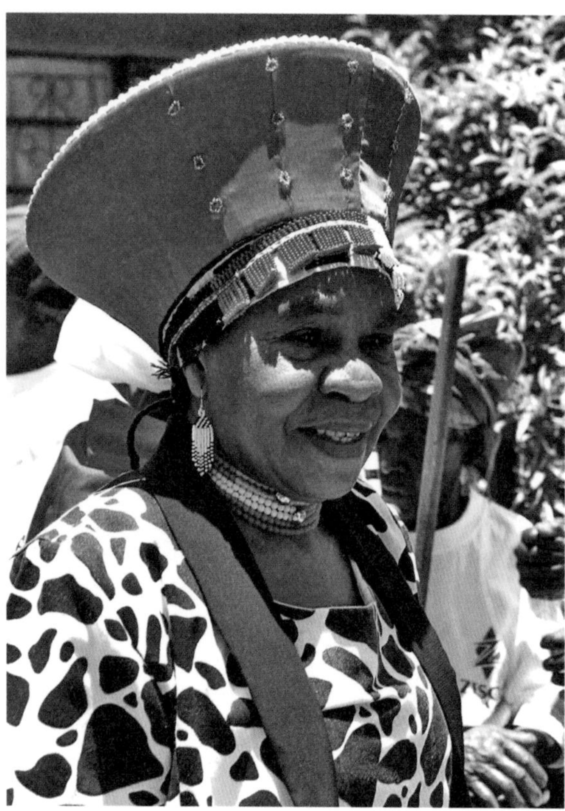

Portrait of Her Royal Highness Chieftainess Nkomeshya Mukamambo II (Name: Elizabeth Mulenje) at Chakwela Makumbi Ceremony to celebrate the beginning of the planting season for the Soli community (the indigenous people of Lusaka province), October 2013

where it has become difficult to travel, I have ended up collaborating with more people which in itself is a form of caring collectively. I have had to film with friends, collaborate with family, finish and install the work partly in absence with the help of the Künstlerhaus Bethanien team and colleagues. The project has been realised through a collective effort, and it has expanded to include views that are not necessarily important only for the Zambian and Zimbabwean contexts.

... these gestures of memory at Künstlerhaus Bethanien has three installations. The first one is the multi-channel I have mentioned earlier, the second one features black flag poles with bark cloth hanging from them in the same way that flags are lowered during national mourning. The third installation is titled *... these wreaths are laid in honour of her memories* and is made of flowers and swings. It can be argued that each one of the installations draws from a gesture of memory.

FM: I feel that in the project *...these gestures of memory* there is a complex and carefully curated conflation of notions about mourning, invoking memories, pain and at the same time celebration. The seaming together of the rich research material and art making is quite impeccable. Was this easy to do?

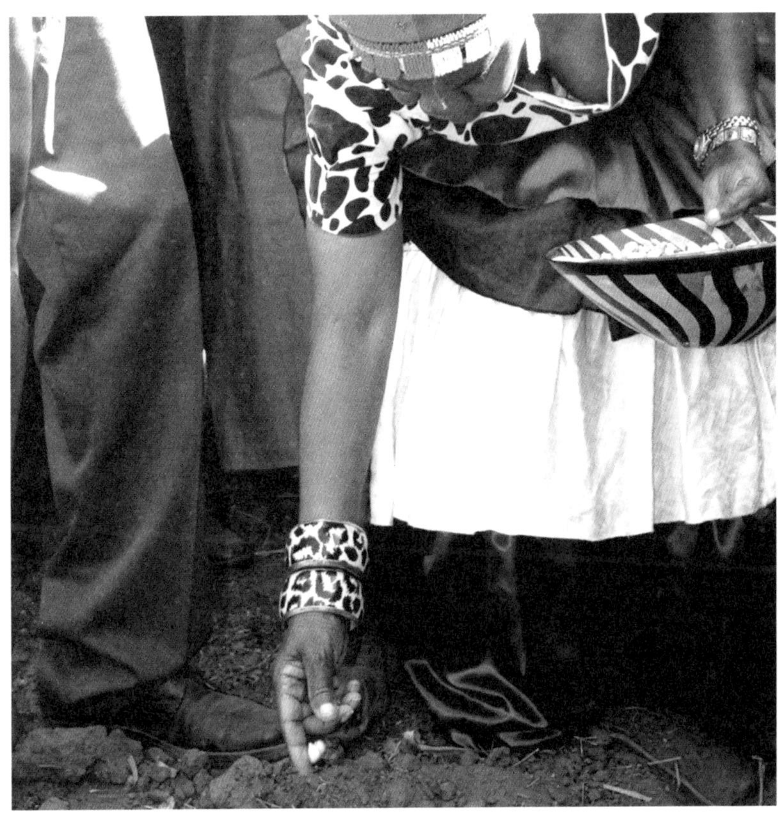

Her Royal Highness Chieftainess Nkomeshya Mukamambo II at Chakwela Makumbi Ceremony, 2013

GK: I am honestly not quite sure if I am able to quantify in terms of easy or hard, I can speak in terms of dedication and genuinely being curious about stories of women freedom fighters. For me the work started by being curious about Chikamoneka's history, I embarked on a journey many years back to find out more about her, along the way I encountered more women. I have had some rather interesting experiences in hearing, seeing and sharing these stories and learning also so much from different collaborators along the way. There have been some successes in unveiling some of these histories and some difficulties in retrieving certain memories. I am unable to make some memories visible, or record each and every single woman's story I have encountered, I am on the fence because it is important for me to acknowledge that these stories, just like the women whom they are based on, have their own urgency. So yes, there are some stories that give cause for celebration. And there are the others: this work can merely serve as a sombre homage to them.

Burial: Erasing Erasure, 2017

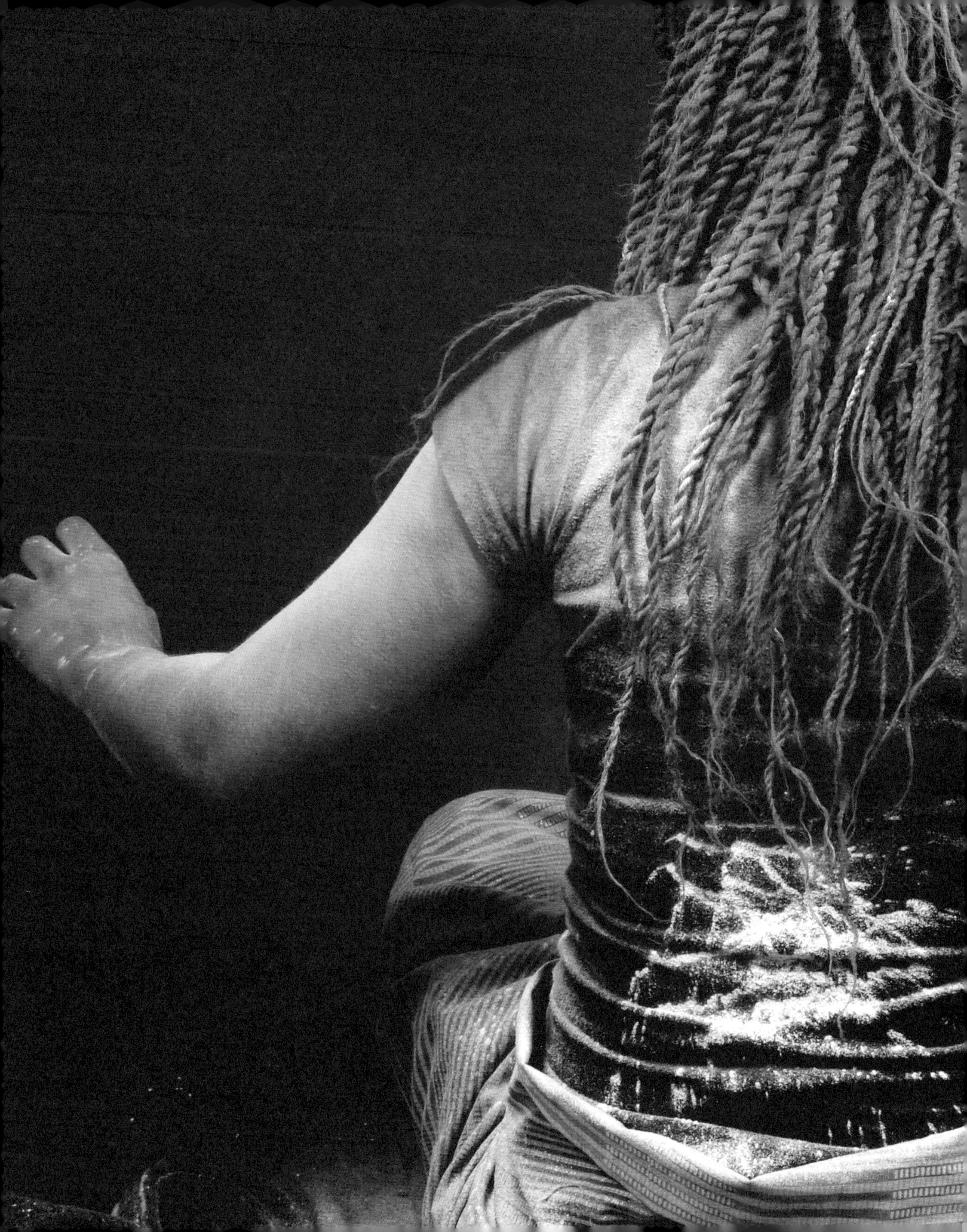

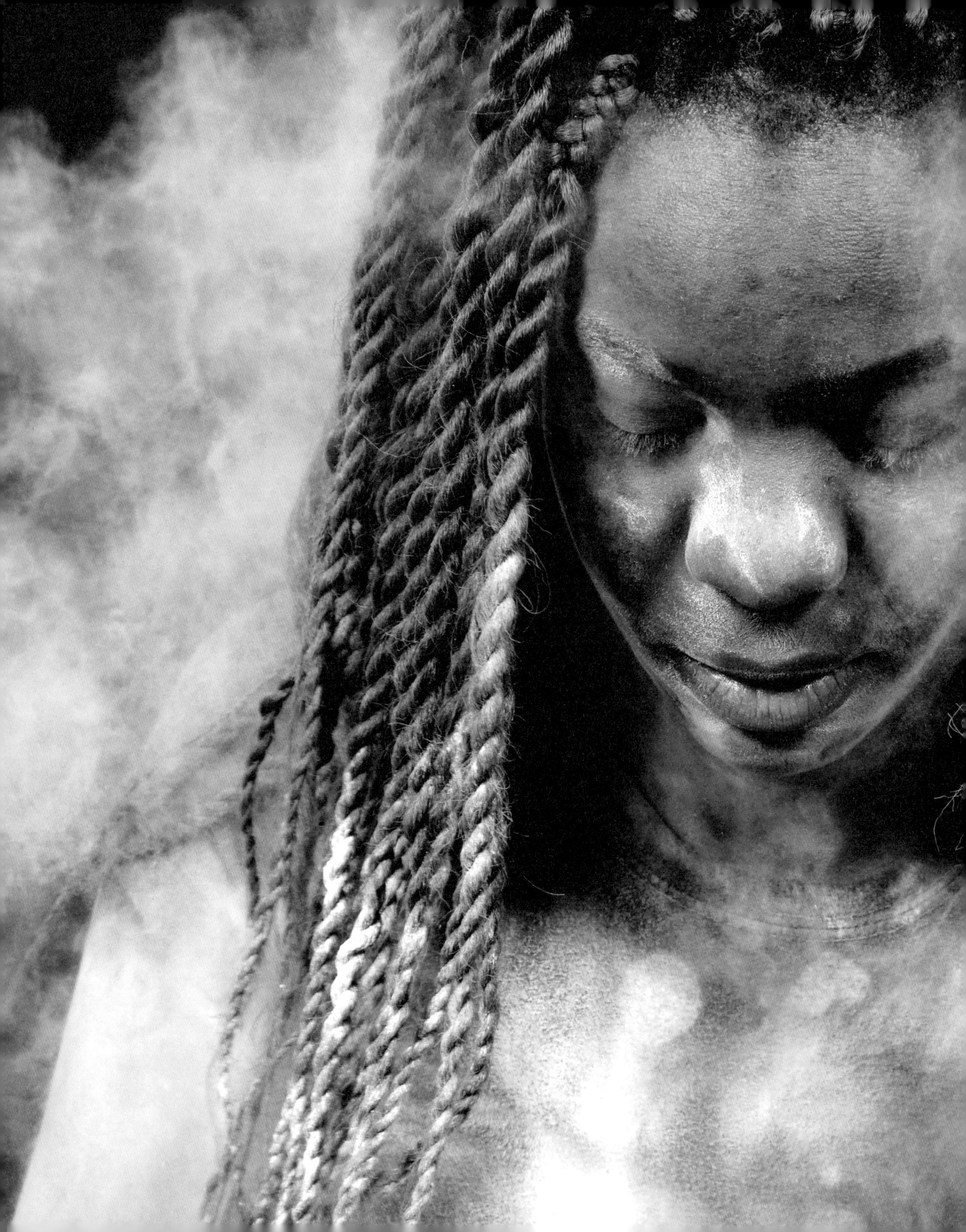

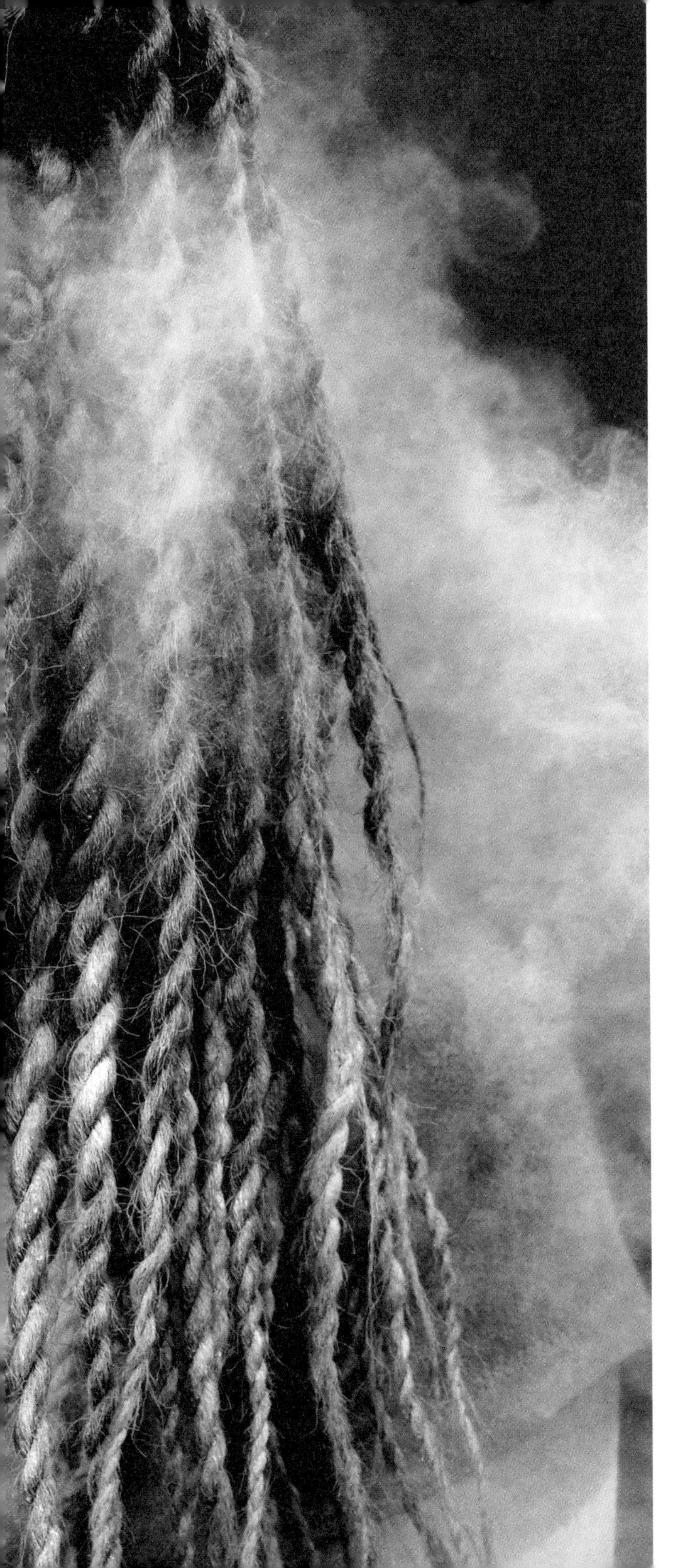

Burial: Erasing Erasure, 2017

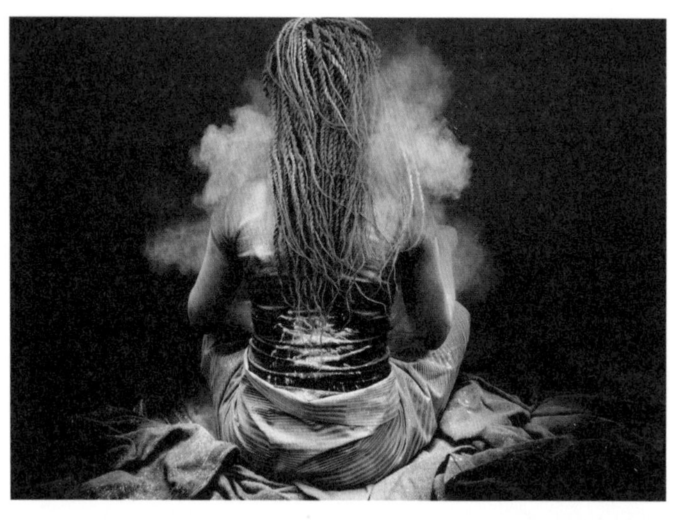
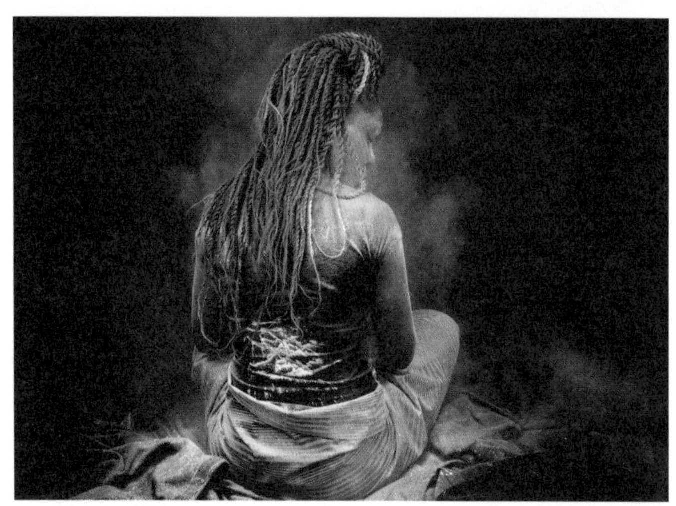
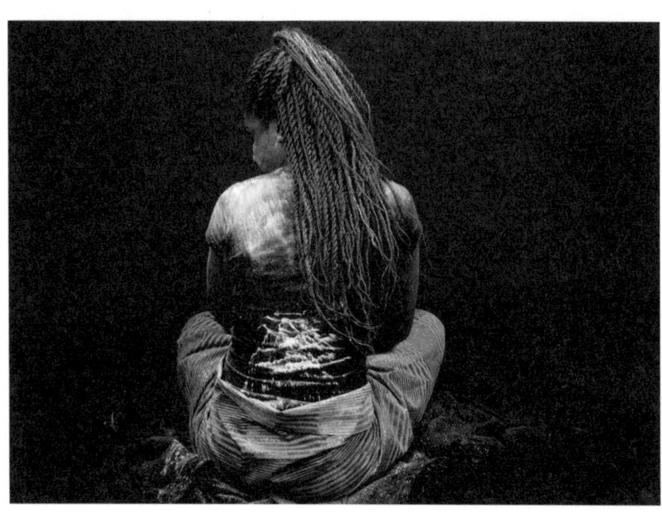
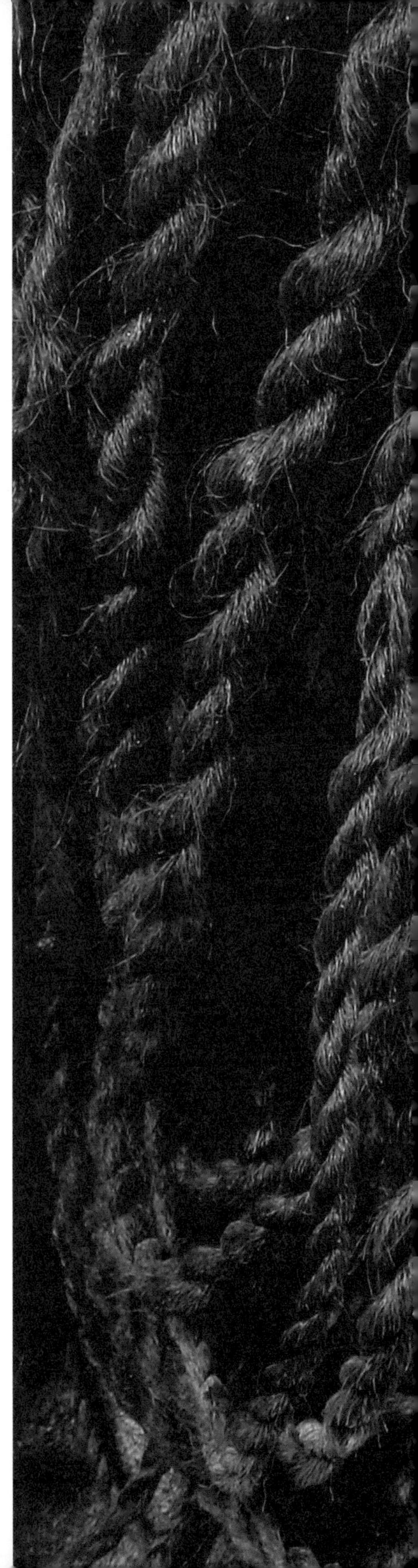

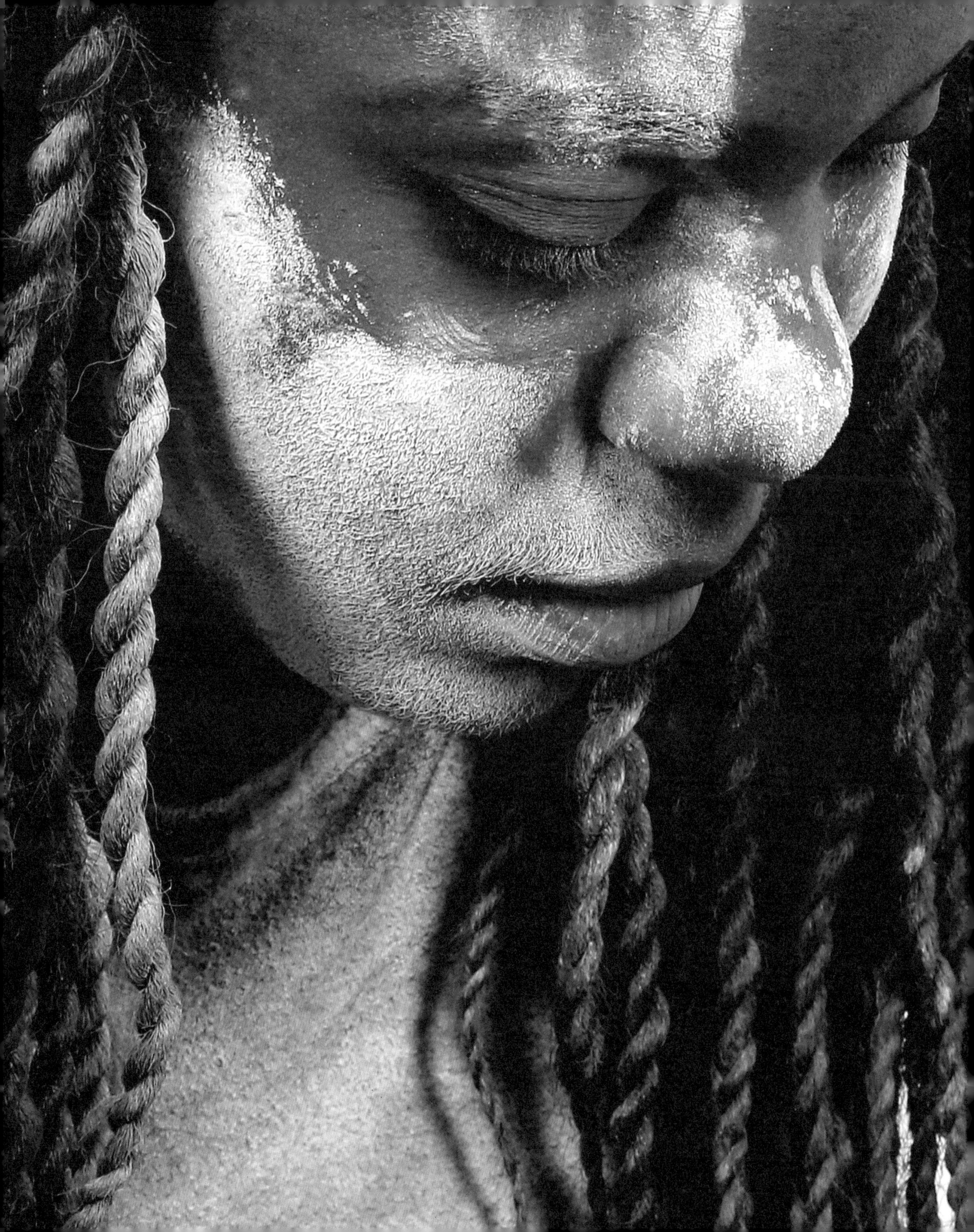

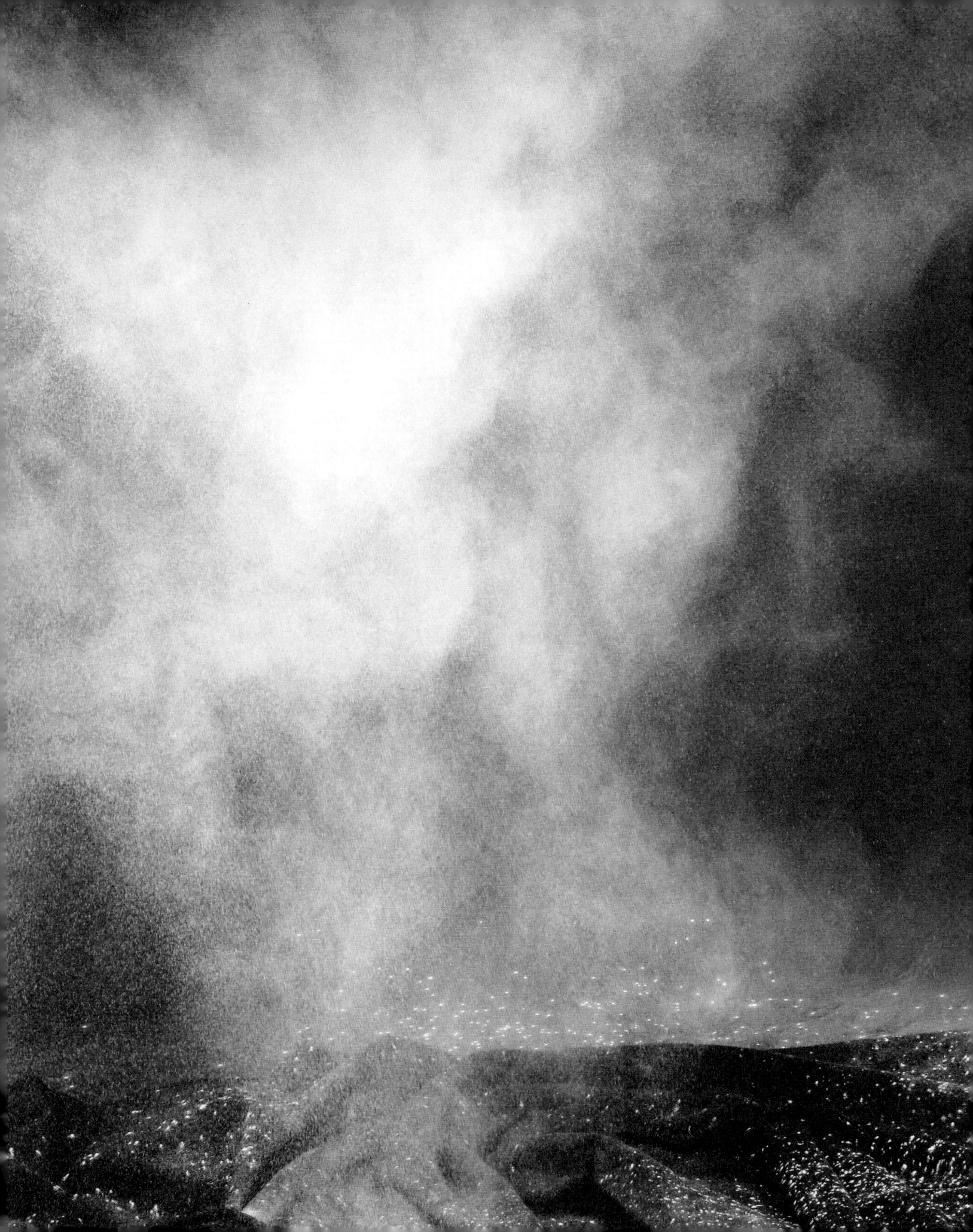

Unburying this narrative, 2017

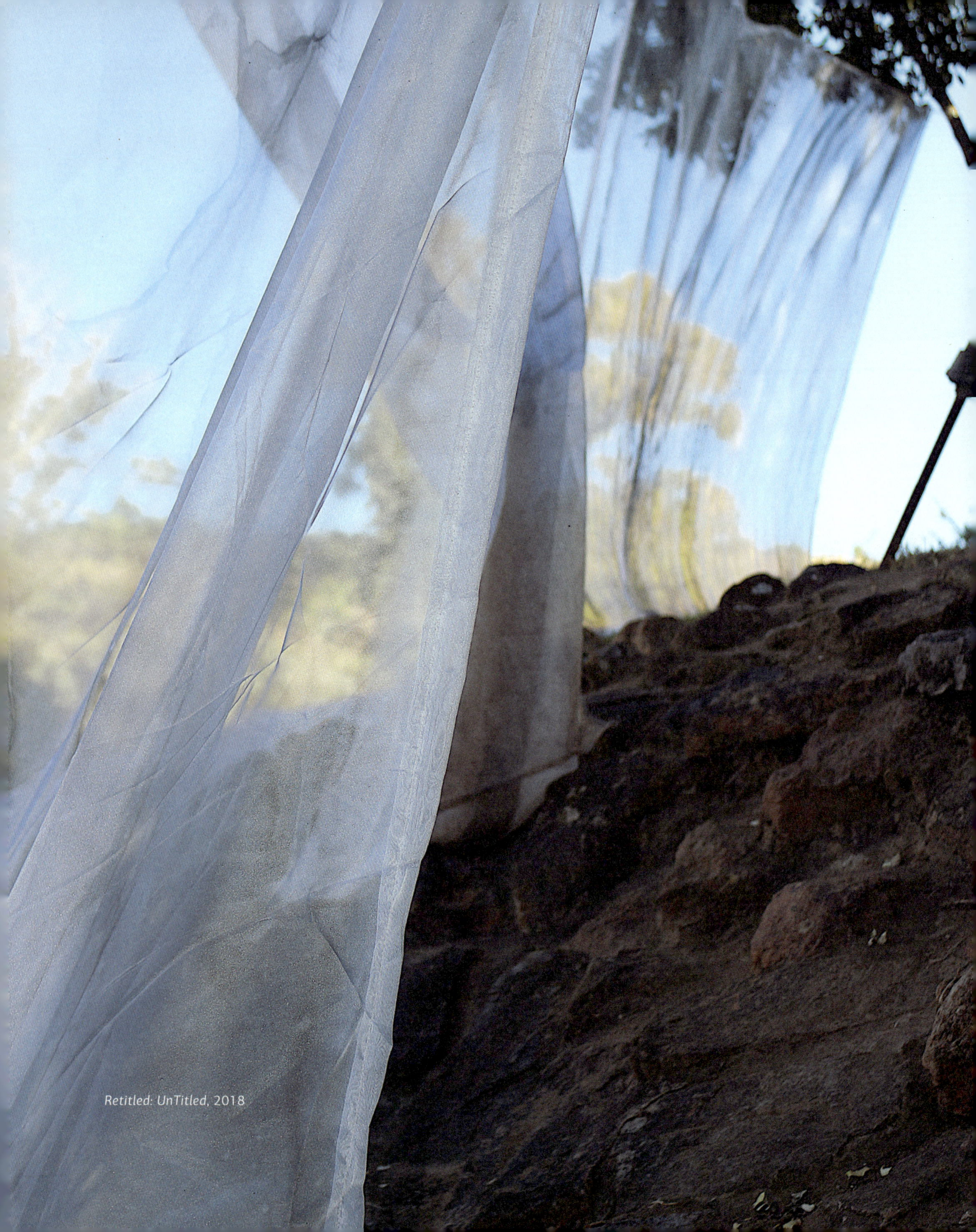

Retitled: UnTitled, 2018

Testures of Erasure: Sidelined Stories of a Marginalised Narrative

Annett Busch

We walked down Cairo Road. We just wanted the white man, particularly Roy Welensky (the Premier of Central Africa) to know that African people were the only people who could build their own nation, not them to build the nation for us.[1]
Julia Chikamoneka, 1961

Thank God for the visual; it takes me away from this quite organized way of thinking and moves me to talk about what a painting can do.
Gladys Kalichini, 2018

Bold was one of the words that came to my mind when I began to understand what Gladys Kalichini aims to realise, which is nothing less than to challenge and shift the parameters of an economy of attention. Her large-scale, multi-layered installations confront us with the ways we see and listen, analyse how we value something and investigate whether we are willing to take the time to understand, whether we dare to care.

As an artist, Kalichini approaches the reverse side of terms – scratching and questioning the surfaces, creating new ones, marking gaps – triggered by her work as a researcher. Kalichini began to explore the lives of Julia Chikamoneka (1910–1986) and Alice Lenshina (1920–1978) in 2014/15, both important figures of the liberation struggles in Zambia in the early 1960s. When she became aware of their absence in the national archives, she embarked on a long journey of questioning the dominant narrative of national histories and the omission of women from them, examining today's concepts of remembrance or rather, how the non-remembering is produced. Like erasure. What does it actually mean to erase, completely, until all traces are gone? Assuming that our ability to imagine change is influenced by our knowledge of the past, how does this lack of knowledge reduce our ability to imagine a changing future?

1 Quoted from Gladys Kalichini, *Fya Moneka: exploring the erasure of women within Zambian history* (Rhodes University, 2018), http://hdl.handle.net/10962/63186. Kalichini quotes from Gisela Geisler, *Women and the Remaking of Politics in Southern Africa: Negotiating Autonomy, Incorporation, and Representation* (Nordic Africa Institute, 2004), accessible via http://www.diva-portal.org; Geisler refers to an interview "Mama UNIP Dies", in *Times of Zambia* (Lusaka), June 21, 1986. In Geisler's book the sentence reads: "We walked naked down Cairo Road." Another history around "nakedness" comes into play here. In a moment of confrontation with Roy Welensky, the protesting women led by Julia Chikamoneka undressed spontaneously as an ultimate act of self-empowerment and outrage. This specific moment of undressing, captured as photography, became the centre of attention whenever the story was later mediated as "naked protest". "Nakedness" turned into a spectacle which in the end covered up the story of Julia Chikamoneka and the complexity of the dynamics and efforts of organising protest, of women's politics and of their struggles for autonomy. Kalichini omits the word "naked" in her quote in order to create a shift of attention, which in turn is closely linked to her artistic practice and aesthetics, to unfreeze the moment of photographic fixation and keep the stories in flux.

To call Kalichini's practice bold describes the way she responds to the challenging and ambiguous endeavour of archival research in Zimbabwe and Zambia. Archival findings construct the larger puzzle of history and, at the same time, always remain incomplete. Hence, they also have the potential to provide information about the conditions and interests of preservation, revealing what is considered to be worthy of preservation and what is not. Within the discourse around archives, Kalichini carries out a double movement as an artist-researcher: she not only asserts the significance of archives as political spaces and the significance of women's stories in particular, but she also detaches her artistic practice from archival appearances, from what is left behind as documentary traces, such as newspaper clippings and – sometimes violent or traumatising – photographs. Kalichini strives for abstraction. She doesn't unveil or reconstruct historical traces, nor does she communicate her way of reading and interpreting: against the impossibility of making the layers of history visible, she creates a completely new aesthetic narrative through abstract colour surfaces, textures and fabric. A form, an outline may refer to the position of a corpse that has been murdered (*UnCovering Silences of the Hidden, and the Unfamiliar*, 2016), or to a female figure claiming the right for her independence (*A Spectacle of Erasure – Her Present Absence*, 2017). A story is set free under new conditions of narration. All decisions concerning the material and the time the artist spends on the process of creation are influenced by the awareness and knowledge she has gained through her research. She then takes the liberty of leaving the realm of documentation to transform absence into new existences and to create a new presence.

Eight metres of canvas – that have been stitched on bark cloth – shape the spatial viewing experience of paint, colour and fabric in *Empty Graves – Unarchived Narratives*, 2017. The unique texture of the material transports its own history: "a tradition of fabric de-

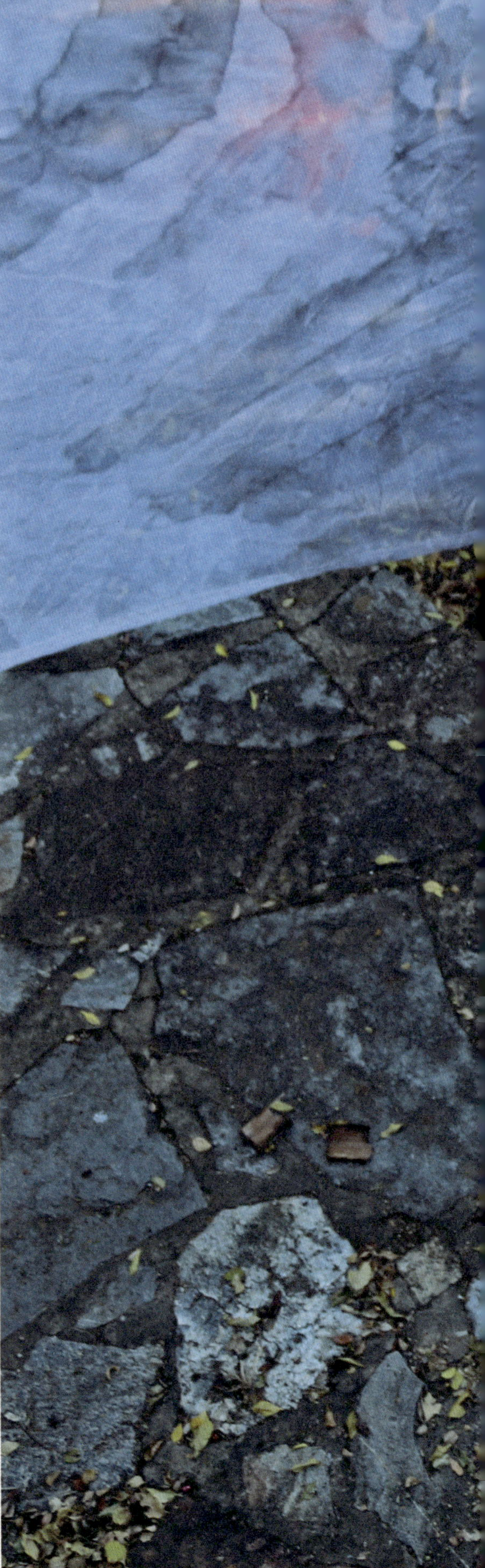

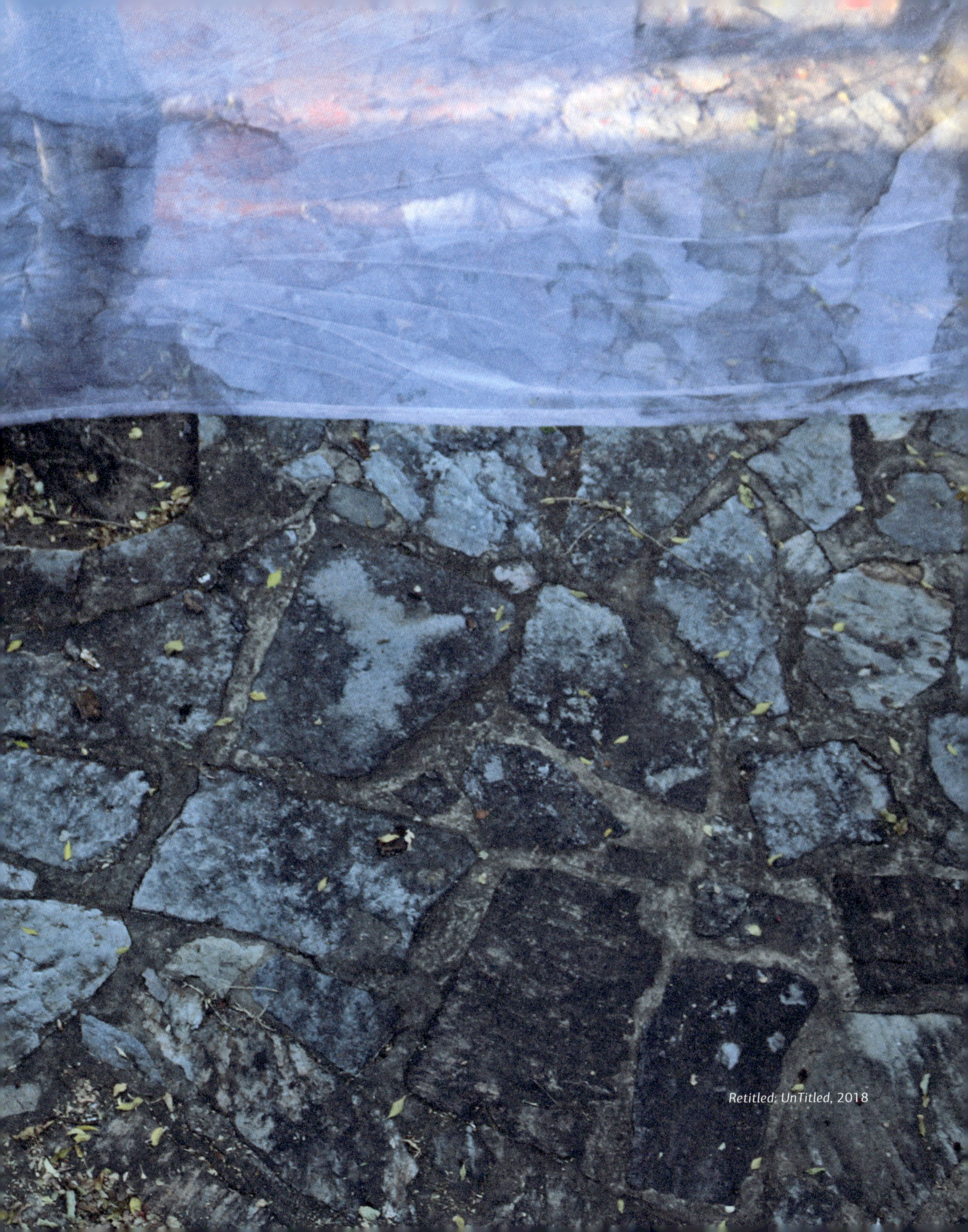

Retitled: UnTitled, 2018

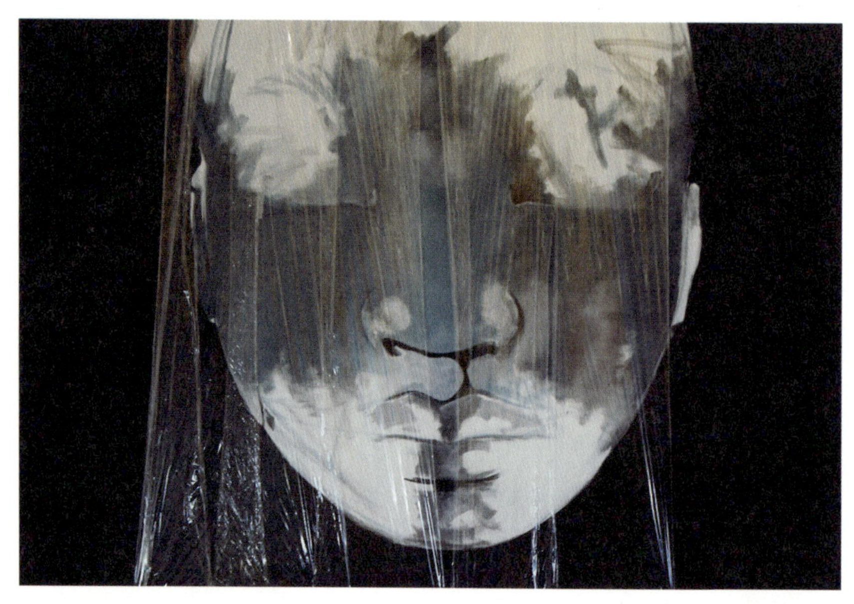

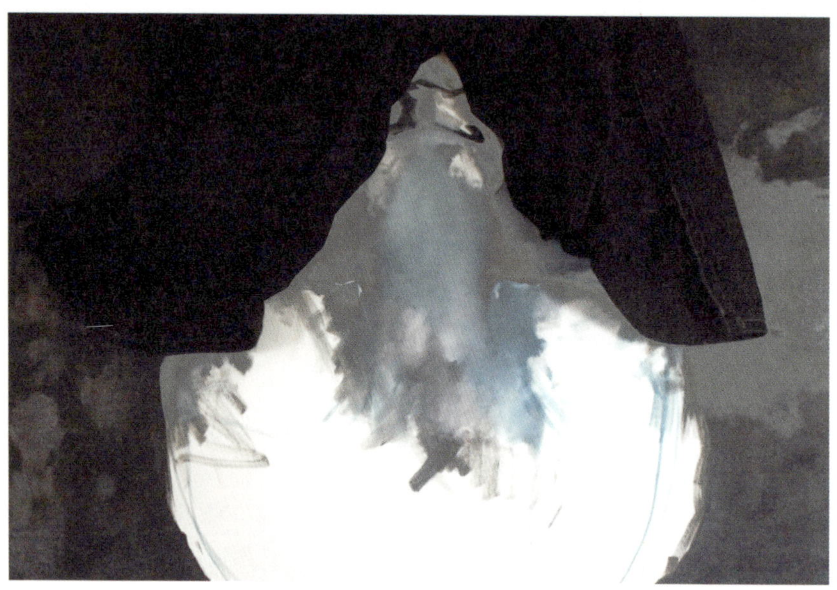

UnCovering Silences of the Hidden, and the Unfamiliar: Mortician's diary I, 2016

sign that predates the technology of weaving".[2] It has been created "by way of stripping, scraping and beating the inner bark of certain plants, most commonly the ficlus species".[3] The production of bark cloth originated in Uganda before it gradually disappeared due to the introduction of cotton cloth by Arab caravan traders in the 19th century. For Kalichini, the use of bark cloth became a symbolic act of forgetting and disappearing: "I use the black bark cloth as burial cloth, just as the Baganda people use it to wrap dead bodies. Decidedly, I do not paint on the bark cloth, but loosely hang it as burial cloth which is no longer wrapped around a corpse to invoke a sense of emptiness, absence and decay of bodies from a grave".[4]

The large format of layered and textured surfaces of canvas and bark cloth create a depth that has the capacity to hold a vacancy for memory. It conjures up unbearable colonial atrocities that cannot actually be seen on a documenting photograph, a picture from the archive. With the theorist Antonio Negri we can think of the multitudes involved whose story will never be represented: "The modern is this abstraction, this participation of the labour of each singularity and its interchangeability. A community which is abstract. [...] The abstract is the sole community in which we exist."[5] When Kalichini addresses histories of women freedom fighters in Zambia and Zimbabwe, like Julia Chikamoneka, Alice Lenshina, Bessie Chibesakunda Kankasa, Mbuya Nehanda or Joice Mujuru, she does not seek to create new heroic narratives. Her aim is to continuously differentiate and enlarge the history and relations around them. In her academic writing, she applies the ideas of the French historian Pierre Nora, referring to his distinction between history and memory and testing how his approach can be adapted and extended within a Zambian and Zimbabwean context. While memory is understood as "a perpetually actual phenomenon, a bond tying us to the eternal present [...] history is a representation of the past. [...] memory is by nature multiple and yet specific; collective, plural, and yet individual."[6]

I got to know Gladys Kalichini through the curator, writer and facilitator Bisi Silva (1962–2019) who passed away so unexpectedly and left a void in the international art world. In 2010, Bisi Silva set up a mobile art school called *Àsìkò* that toured across the African continent from Lagos, Accra, Dakar, Addis Ababa, to Maputo. Bringing together artists, critics and curators for five weeks at a time, it served as a space "to learn how to unlearn",[7] offering the possibility for exchange and a "time out". "*Àsìkò* is a Yoruba word that translates as 'time' in English [...] to explore shifts across temporal registers."[8] Kalichini attended Àsìkò in 2015 in Maputo/Mozambique. Meeting her through Bisi Silva refers to the particular, invaluable connections and fragile, unforeseeable lines which sometimes span continents and build new networks. Such relations are based on the principle of caring: a notion which is all too quickly associated and confused with community work, with labour mostly carried out by women. That is a part of it, but *to care*, daring to care, is much more. It describes

2 Venny Nakazibwe, *Bark-cloth of the Baganda people of Southern Uganda: a record of continuity and change from the late eighteenth century to the early twenty-first century* (Middlesex University, 2005), p. iv., https://eprints.mdx.ac.uk/7008/2/Nakazibwe-phd.pdf.

3 Ibid.

4 Gladys Kalichini in an email conversation with the author, April 18, 2020.

5 Antonio Negri, "Letter to Gianmarco on the Abstract", in *Art and Multitude* (Cambridge, Oxford, Boston, New York: Polity, 2011), pp. 3–12.

6 Pierre Nora, "Between Memory and History: Les Lieux de Mémoire", in *Representations*, no. 26, special issue: *Memory and Counter-Memory* (Spring 1989), p. 9.

7 Bisi Silva, "Creating Space for a Hundred Flowers to Bloom" in *Women on Aeroplanes—Inflight Magazine 4*, p. 6, http://woa.kein.org/inflight04. The text was first published in Silva (ed.), *ÀSÌKÒ: On the Future of Artistic and Curatorial Pedagogies in Africa, Centre for Contemporary Art*, Lagos 2017, pp. xii–xxiii.

8 Ibid.

an intellectual practice or artistic activity which is no less time-consuming; a thought process interconnected by research that pays attention to details, sideways, bifurcations, word and material findings. In this way, it aims to construct a much more populated and complex picture of history. *Caring* can be understood as a mode of resistance, as a counter-concept to erasure, since it is carelessness that ultimately leads to complete erasure, even if traces, pieces, documents still remain. If no one cares about them, they simply don't matter. And as long as historic narratives are not called into question, the present remains a time of poor imagination. Not to care is a violent act, as is erasure. At the same time, the statement "I don't care" is just as important to distinguish what is meaningful to us and what is not. Bisi Silva's pedagogy can be understood in these terms, as well as Gladys Kalichini's movements as an artist. Their view of artistic creation essentially contradicts commodification, based on an understanding of spending time that is impossible to measure as exchange value in relation to the outcome. To change our economy of attention within a society that is based on the principles of a capitalist economy also means to value the time it needs to *take care* in very different ways.[9]

In her new project that the artist developed during her stay at Künstlerhaus Bethanien in Berlin, she picks up all the threads – archival and material findings, unresolved questions, stories not yet told. During a self-reflexive journey of research, looking at the same thing over and over again, one might even begin to see the blind spots of the story, the sidelined stories of an already marginalised narrative, or what is hidden in plain sight. Kalichini challenges the prevailing narrative of history, focusing on Western power constellations and nation-building and instead visualises global and complex entanglements. With the focus on the role of women's stories, she not only highlights the few who have made

9 See for example Mariana Mazzucato, *The Value of Everything* (London: Penguin Books, 2019).

UnCovering Silences of the Hidden, and the Unfamiliar: Mortician's diary II, 2016

it into the books as heroines, but also includes the web, the community – it may take a while before one sees the big picture. For her concept of visibility, Kalichini began to explore the idea of invisibility as described by Ralph Ellison: "I am invisible, understand, simply because people refuse to see me. [...] When they approach me they see only my surroundings, themselves, or figments of their imagination – indeed, everything and anything except me."[10]

With her current project, Kalichini looks at types of mourning to unveil how women's stories are commemorated. She has spent much time multiplying these untold stories, folding a large number of flowers with black crepe paper until they became an "ephemeral monument".[11] The double function of mourning is to overcome the pain of loss, to give the pain enough time and space, however, not (only) to forget, but to transform pain into remembrance, into a new presence – a process which must always remain incomplete and selective.

10 *Invisible Man* is a novel by Ralph Ellison, published by Random House in 1952.

11 Gladys Kalichini in an email conversation with the author, May 11, 2020.

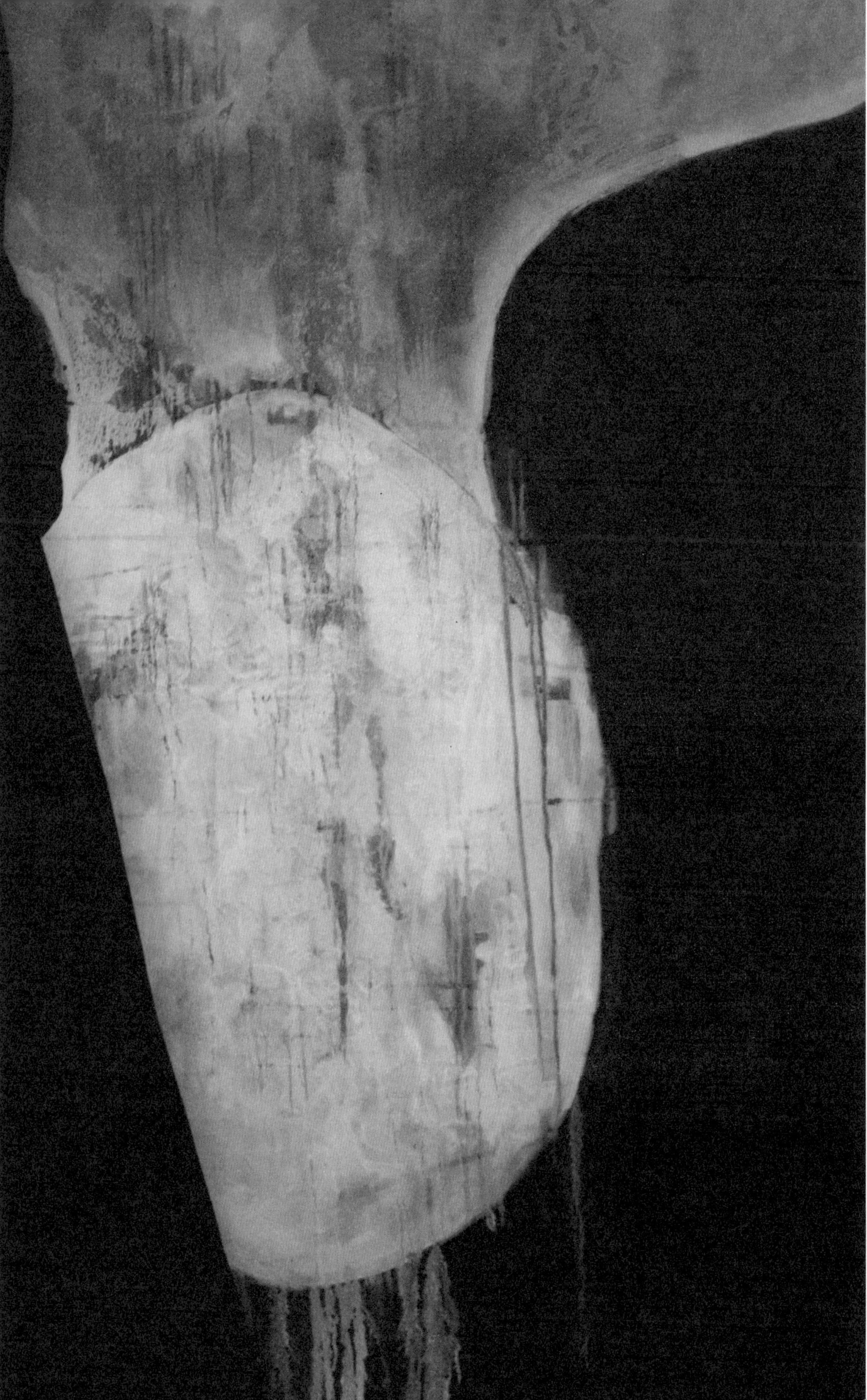

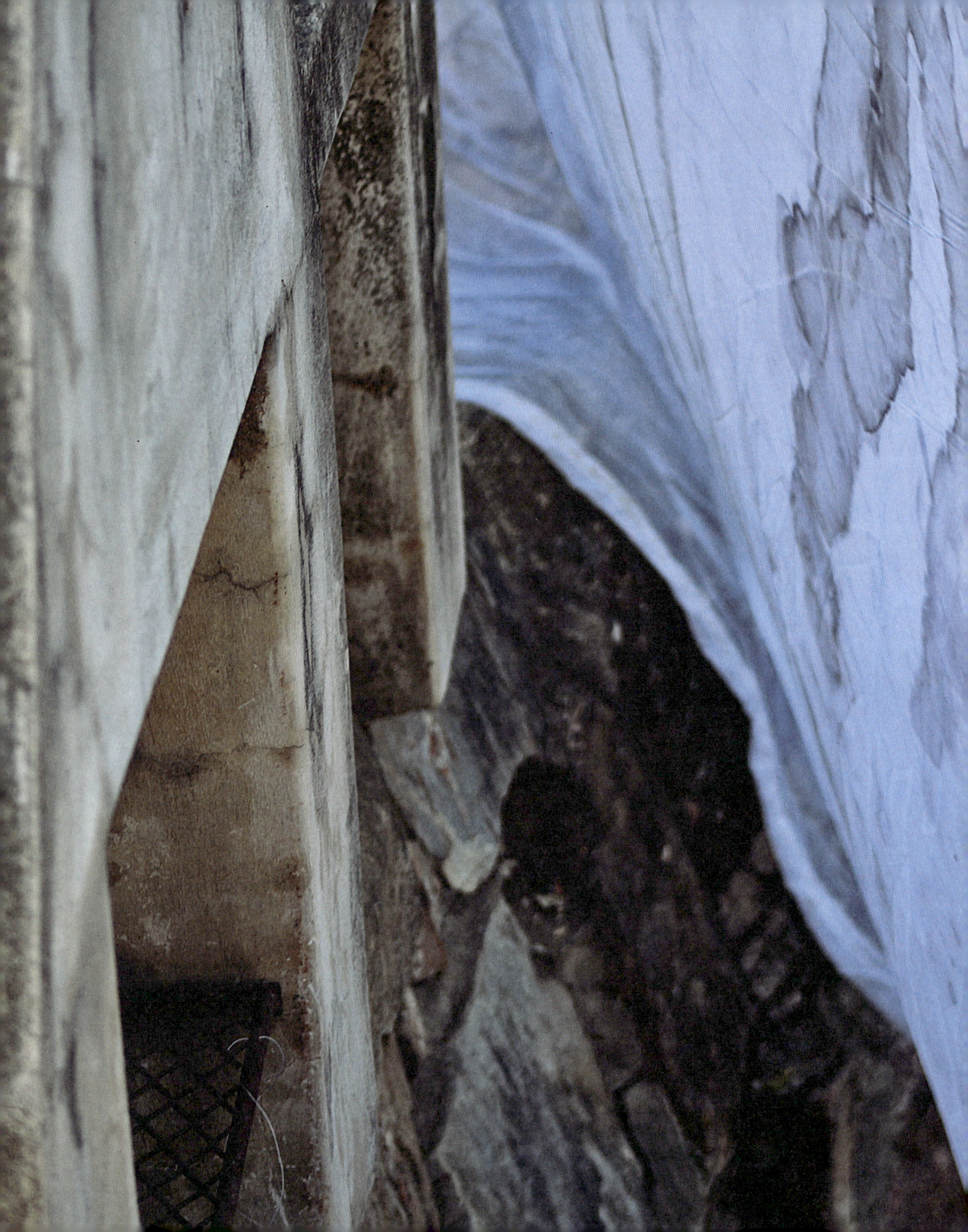

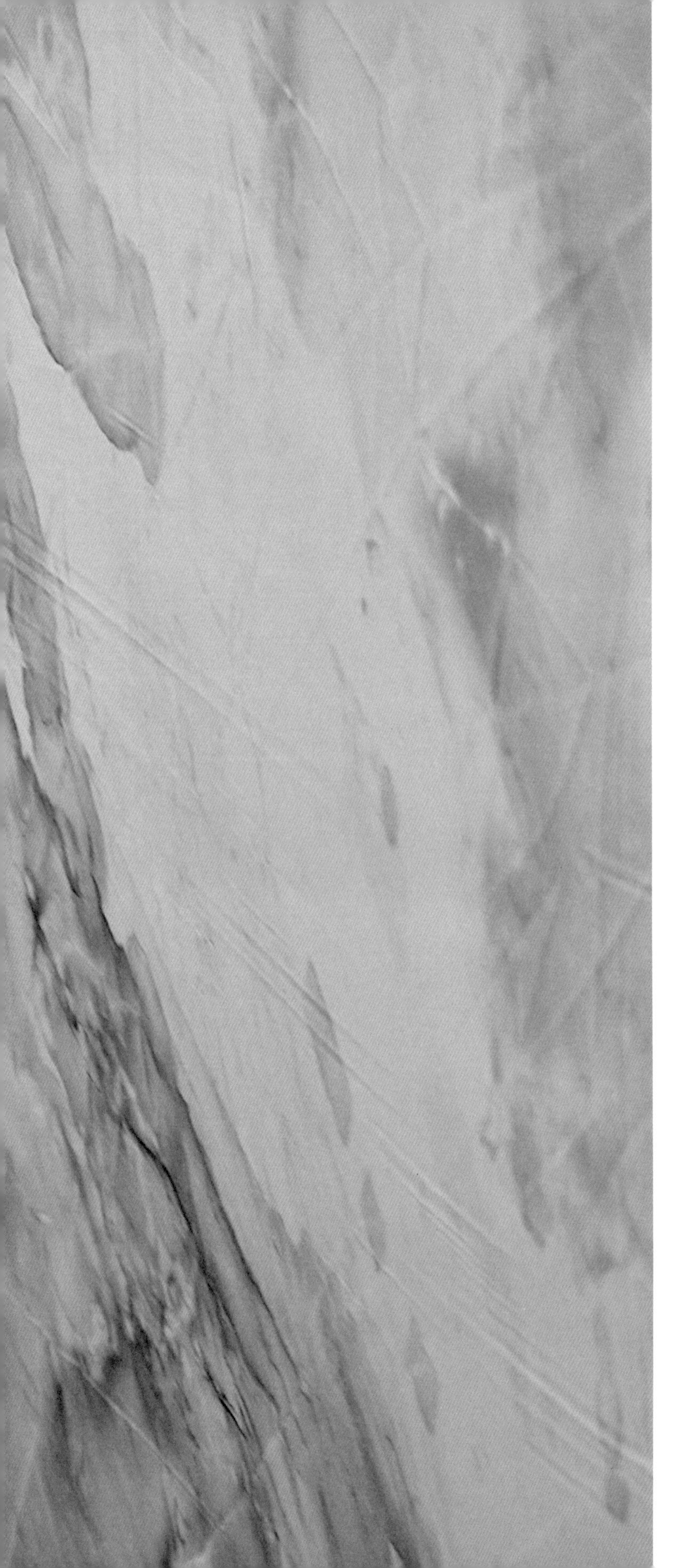

Retitled: UnTitled, 2018

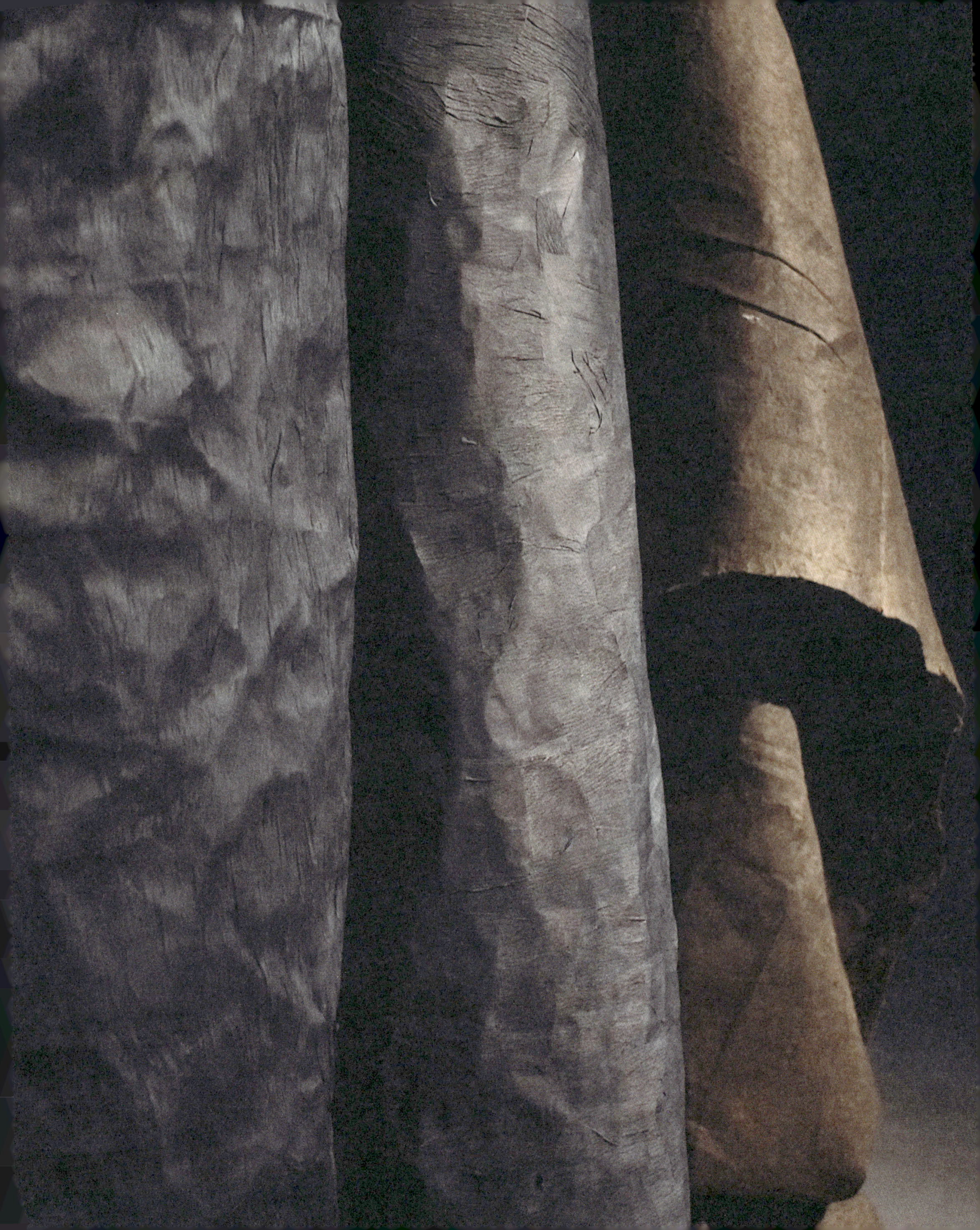

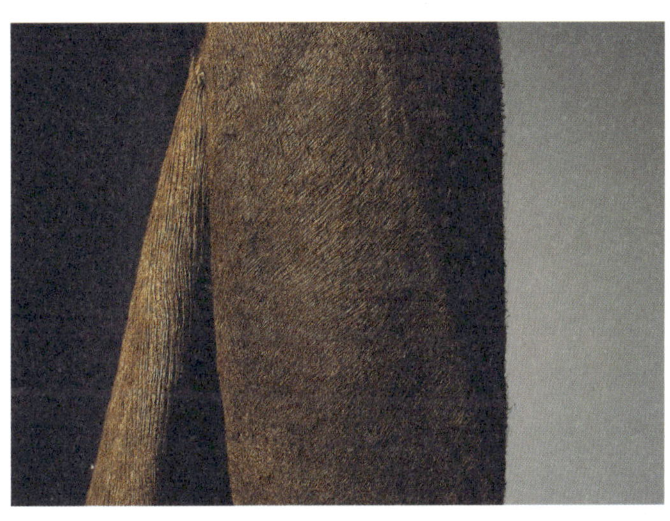

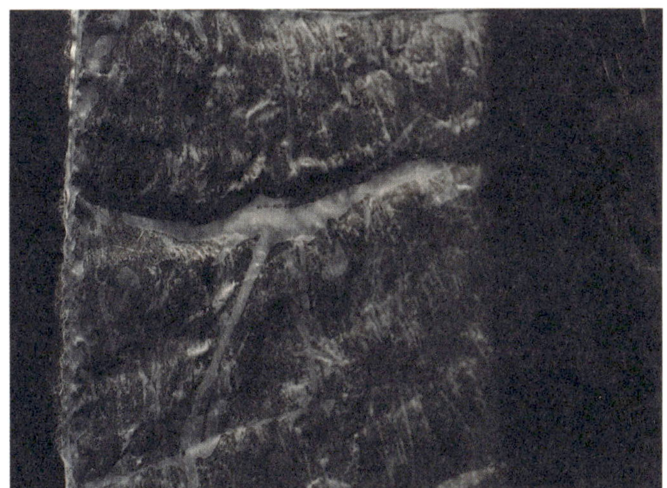

…these moments are spent seeing her invisibility and hearing her silence,
2019–2020

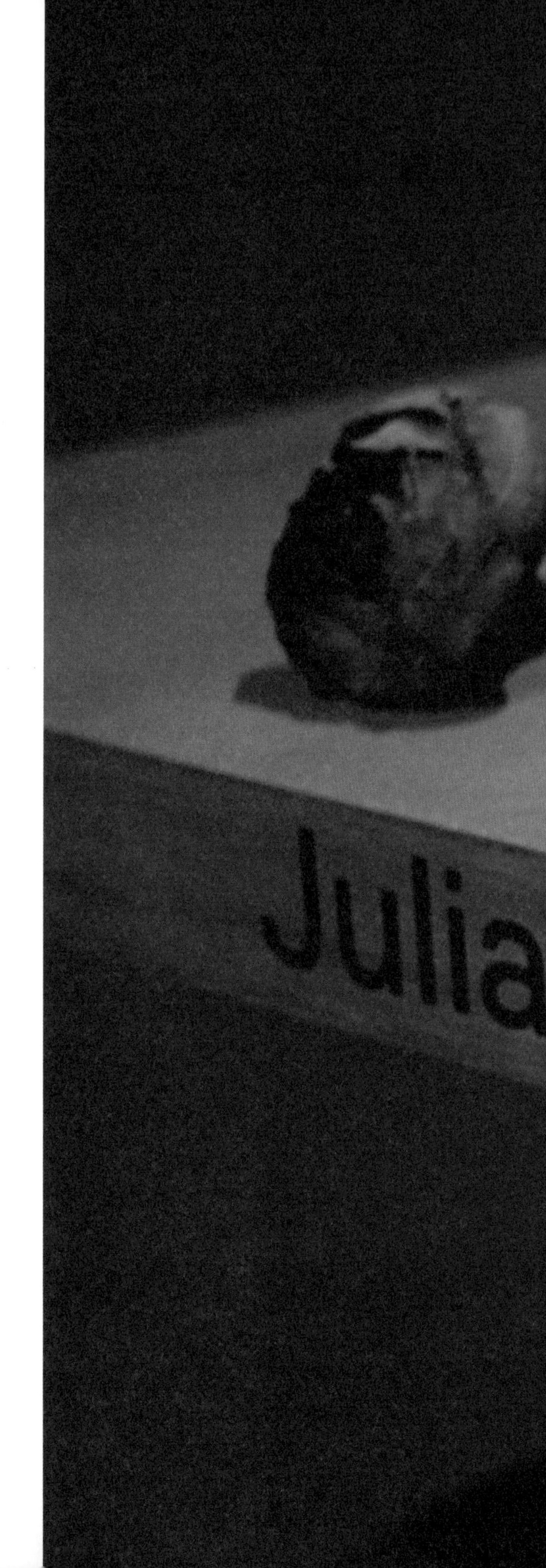

...these wreaths are laid in honour of her memories, 2020

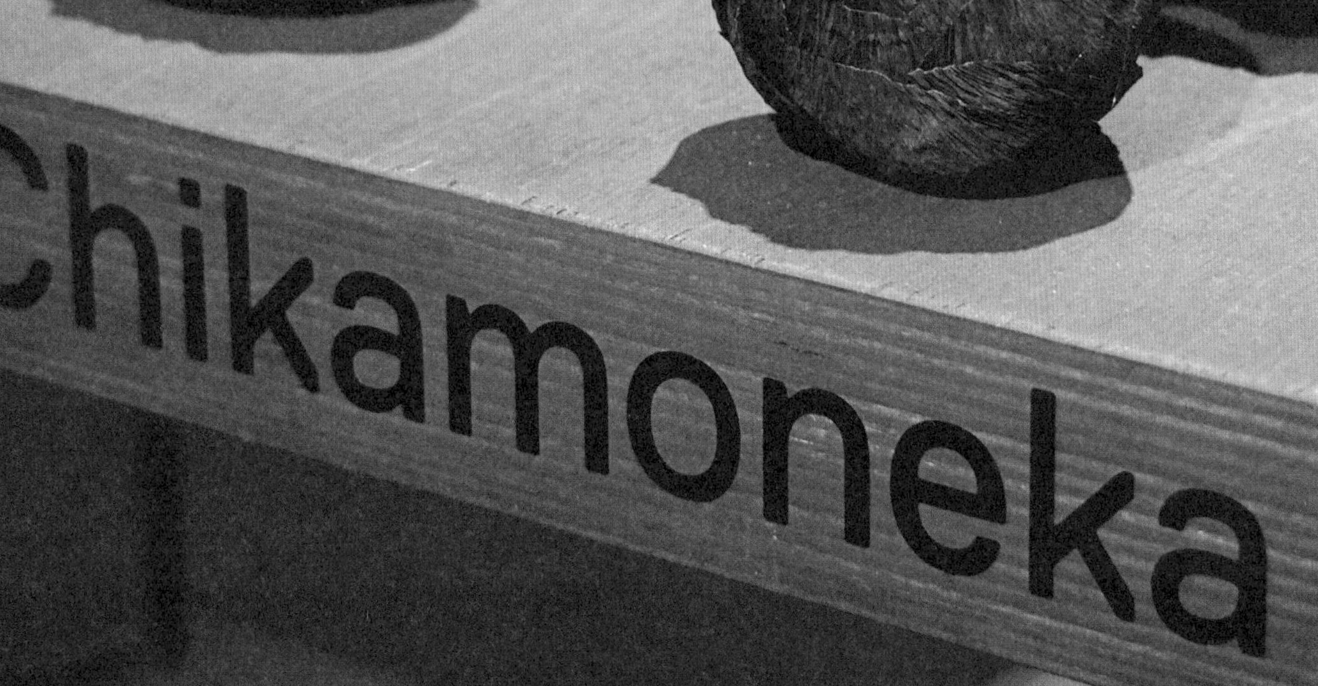
Chikamoneka

List of Images

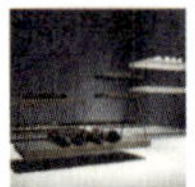 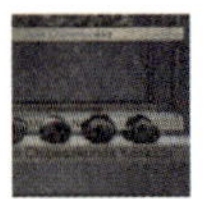 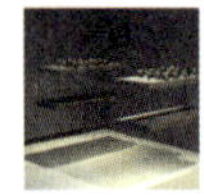

...these wreaths are laid in honour of her memories, 2020, wood, string and paper, dimensions variable, © Künstlerhaus Bethanien/Peter Rosemann

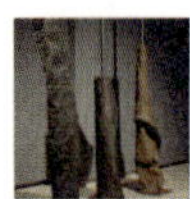

...these moments are spent seeing her invisibility and hearing her silence, 2019–2020, bark cloths and paper on voile, dimensions variable, © Künstlerhaus Bethanien/David Brandt

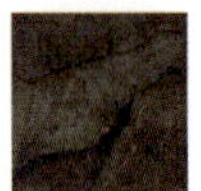

untitled, 2020, fabric and paper on canvas, dimensions variable, © Gladys Kalichini

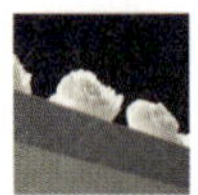 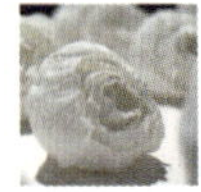 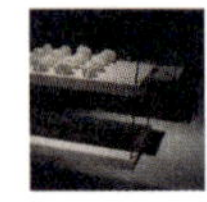

...these wreaths are laid in honour of her memories, 2020, wood, string and paper, dimensions variable, © Gladys Kalichini/Arthur Debert

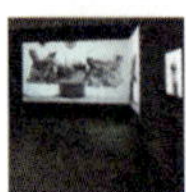

...these practices are done in sharing her stories, 2020, four-channel video installation, 04:20 min, loop, © Gladys Kalichini/Arthur Debert

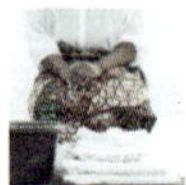 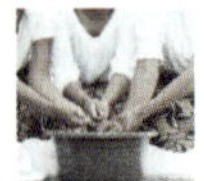 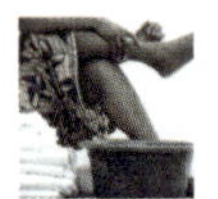

...these practices are done in sharing her stories, 2020, four-channel video installation, 04:20 min, loop, video stills, © Gladys Kalichini

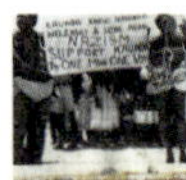 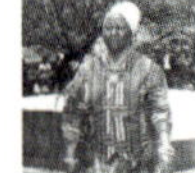 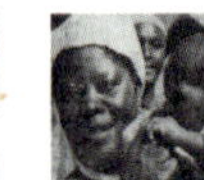 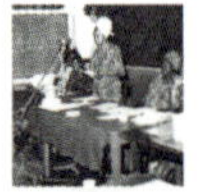 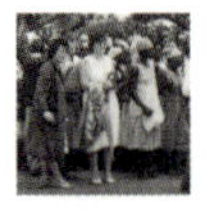 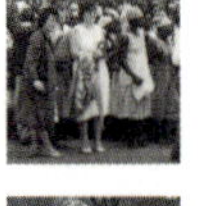

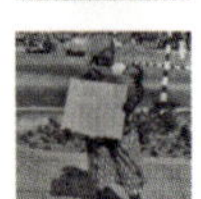 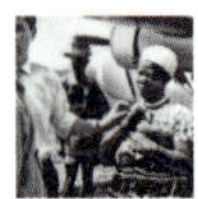 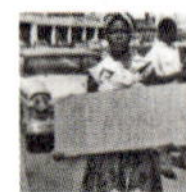 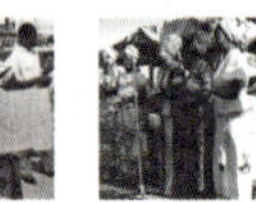 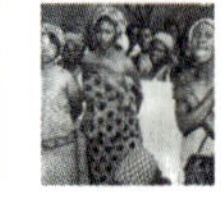

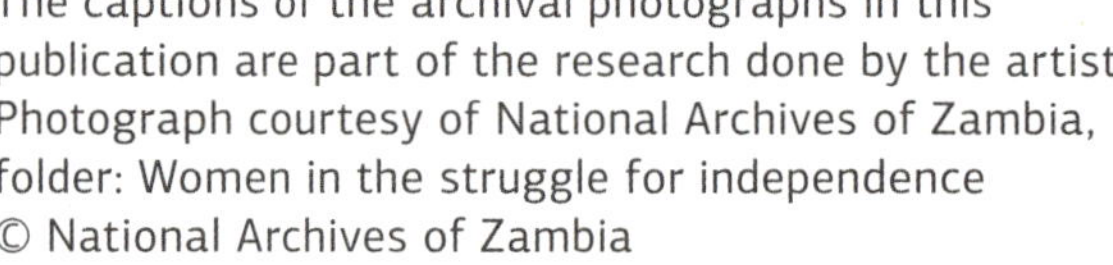

The captions of the archival photographs in this publication are part of the research done by the artist. Photograph courtesy of National Archives of Zambia, folder: Women in the struggle for independence © National Archives of Zambia

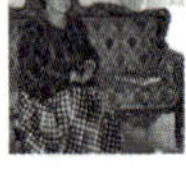

Bessie Chibeskakunda Kankasa, 2016, © Gladys Kalichini

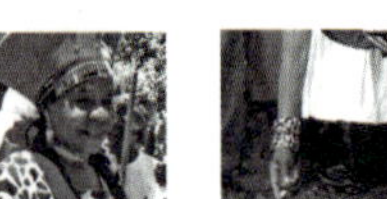

Her Royal Highness Chieftainess Nkomeshya Mukamambo II, 2013, © Andrew Mulenga

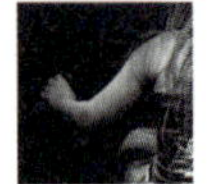 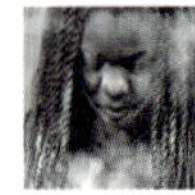 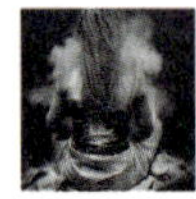 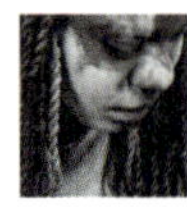

Burial: Erasing Erasure, 2017, video, 04:05 min, stills, © Gladys Kalichini

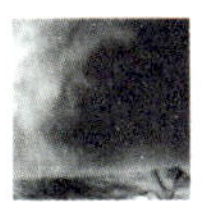

Unburying this narrative, 2017, video, 03:00 min, still, © Gladys Kalichini

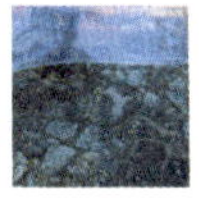
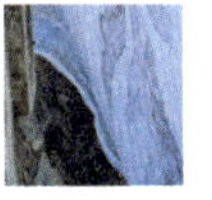

Retitled: UnTitled, 2018, ink on voile, dimensions variable, © Gladys Kalichini

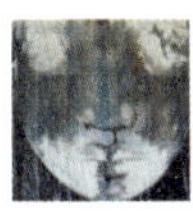
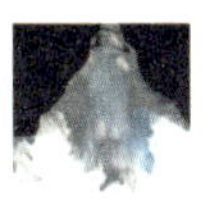

UnCovering Silences of the Hidden, and the Unfamiliar: Mortician's diary I, 2016, painting and fabric, 150 cm x 250 cm, © Gladys Kalichini

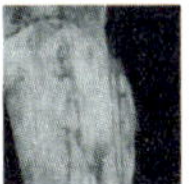

UnCovering Silences of the Hidden, and the Unfamiliar: Mortician's diary II, 2016, painting and fabric, 250 cm x 150 cm, © Gladys Kalichini

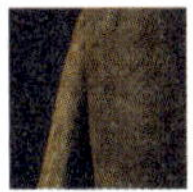
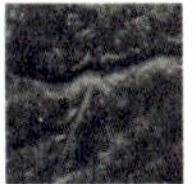
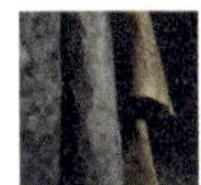

...these moments are spent seeing her invisibility and hearing her silence, 2019–2020, bark cloths and paper on voile, dimensions variable, © Gladys Kalichini/Arthur Debert

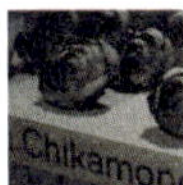

...these wreaths are laid in honour of her memories, 2020, wood, string and paper, dimensions variable, © Gladys Kalichini/Arthur Debert

Biography

Gladys Kalichini
Born 1989 in Chingola, Zambia
Lives and works in Lusaka/Zambia and Grahamstown/South Africa

EDUCATION

2017–20 PhD Candidate: Art History and Visual Culture, Rhodes University, Grahamstown/South Africa
Scholarship by Andrew W. Mellon Foundation (2018–2020)

2017 Master of Fine Art, Rhodes University, Grahamstown

2013 Bachelor of Arts (Economics), The University of Zambia, Lusaka

RESIDENCIES

2019–20 Artist-in-residence programme of KfW Stiftung at Künstlerhaus Bethanien, Berlin

2017 Fountainhead Residency, supported by African Artists in Residency Centre's programme, Miami/USA

SELECTED EXHIBITIONS

2021 ***Talya Lubinsky and Gladys Kalichini***, Villa 102, Frankfurt

2020 12th Bienal do Mercosul, Porto Alegre/Brazil
… these gestures of memory, Künstlerhaus Bethanien, Berlin (Solo)

2019 ***And Counting***, Johannesburg Art Gallery, Johannesburg/South Africa

2018 ***Converge***, Rawspot Gallery, Grahamstown
Exhuming Histories, National Gallery, Livingstone/Zambia
art summit, experimental pavilion, Lagos/Nigeria
The Last Image Show, Alliance Francaise, Lusaka and Dar Es Salaam/Tanzania

2017 ***Chamoneka: UnCasting Shadows***, Grahamstown (Solo)
Dakar experimental pavilion, Gallery of small things, Dakar/Senegal
Ingwe, Rhodes Fine Art Department, Grahamstown

2015 ***28 Words in Maputo***, Forteleza, Maputo/Mozambique

2012 ***Crossing Borders***, Emergent Art Space, San Francisco/USA
National Exhibition, Henry Tayali Gallery, Lusaka

2011 ***Black History Month Meets Women's Day***, Henry Tayali Gallery, Lusaka

2010 ***Independence Exhibition***, Henry Tayali Gallery, Lusaka
Women's exhibition "equal rights and opportunities" and ***Black History Heroes and Heroines***, Lusaka National Museum, Lusaka

SEMINARS AND PRESENTATIONS

2019 ***From Studio to Post-studio-practice***, with Yvette Mutumba, Institut für Kunst im Kontext, Universität der Künste (UdK), Künstlerhaus Bethanien, Berlin

2018 ***Looking For Collete Omogbai, FyaMoneka: Navigating the Erasure of Women in National Archives***, Women On Aeroplanes #2: Search Research, Lagos

2016 ***SArCHI Research Group, Decolonising the Arts – Perspectives From the African Continent***, Grahamstown

2015 ***Àsìkò***, The History of Contemporary Art in Mozambique in 4 weeks, Maputo

2013 ***Insaka Artist's International Workshop***, Cultural Heritage, Livingstone, Zambia

About the Authors:

Annett Busch, based in Trondheim, works as an independent curator, editor, writer, translator and researcher. Her interest in radical forms of filmmaking and film criticism led to the publications *Ousmane Sembène – Interviews* (University Press of Mississippi, co-edited with Max Annas, 2008), *Frieda Grafe: 30 Filme* (Brinkmann & Bose, 2013, together with Max Annas and Henriette Gunkel) and the exhibition and book *Matters of Collaboration* (Akademie der Künste, Berlin, 2017 / Sternberg Press, 2020, together with Tobias Hering). She co-designed *After Year Zero – Geographies of Collaboration*, a series of cross-disciplinary workshops in various cities in Africa and Europe (2012–13, funded by the Goethe-Institut). In addition, she co-curated the exhibition *Electronic Textures* at Haus der Kulturen der Welt, Berlin, 2013, and at the Museum of Modern Art in Warsaw, 2015, and co-edited the accompanying reader (all with Anselm Franke). From 2016 to 2019, Busch managed and curated the collaborative artistic research project *Electronic Textures* at KIT (Trondheim Academy of Fine Art) which set up a virtual research laboratory and exhibition platform for pan-African magazines. At the same time, she co-initiated and co-curated (with Marie-Hélène Gutberlet, Magda Lipska and The Otolith Collective) the ongoing international research, exhibition and publishing project *Women on Aeroplanes* together with institutional partners in Berlin, London, Lagos, Warsaw, Bayreuth and Johannesburg.

Fadzai Veronica Muchemwa is a researcher, writer and emerging curator working in Harare, Zimbabwe. She is the Curator for Education and Public Programming at the National Gallery of Zimbabwe and a collaborator for Independent Curators International and the Zimbabwe Pavilion at the International Art Exhibition in Venice. Muchemwa's research explores the history and memory of African storytelling, new communities of protest and transgression, histories of cities, topographies of knowledge production and sites of transition. She is also interested in the diaspora and how it shapes the social fabric of the continent as well as how the global North has influenced trends in Africa. Muchemwa has co-curated *Culture in Communities* (National Gallery of Zimbabwe, 2016), *Jazzified: Expressions of Protest and Moulding a Nation: The History of the Ceramics Collection of the National Gallery of Zimbabwe* (National Gallery of Zimbabwe, 2018–2019), and *Dis(colour)ed Margins* (National Gallery of Zimbabwe, 2017). In addition, she curated *The Unseen: Creatures of Myth and Legend*, an exhibition of artworks by Isaac Kalambata at the Lusaka National Museum in 2018. Muchemwa took part in the International Training Programme at the British Museum in London and the Glasgow Museums in 2017. She was visiting curator at the Bag Factory Artists' Studios in Johannesburg in 2019 and produced a publication *Curating Johannesburg: rest.less, under siege/in transition*. Muchemwa is a member of the curatorial collective Practice Theory.

Gladys Kalichini – ... these gestures of memory
With an Essay by Annett Busch and a Conversation between Fadzai Muchemwa and Gladys Kalichini

Editors: Daniela Leykam, Christoph Tannert

Künstlerhaus Bethanien GmbH, Kohlfurter Straße 41/43, Showroom: Kottbusser Str. 10, D-10999 Berlin, www.bethanien.de
Artistic Director: Christoph Tannert / **Administrative Director:** Andrea Boche
International Studio Programme: Valeria Schulte-Fischedick / **Press & PR:** Christina Sickert, Carola Uehlken
Administration: Ute Werner / **Technical Staff:** Toni Lebkücher, Peter Rosemann

KfW Stiftung, Palmengartenstraße 5-9, D-60325 Frankfurt am Main, www.kfw-stiftung.de
Executive Director: Dr. Aischa Astou Saw / **Programme Manager Arts and Culture:** Daniela Leykam

Editing: Tomke Braun, Daniela Leykam / **Project Coordination:** Tomke Braun
Copyediting: Aymone Rassaerts
Design: Thorsten Probst / angenehme-gestaltung.de / **Production:** Druckerei Kettler, Bönen
Photos: David Brandt p. 10; Arthur Debert pp. 14–19, 56–59; Gladys Kalichini pp. 11, 20–27, 31, 38–45, 46–50, 35–55; Andrew Mulenga pp. 36–37; National Archives of Zambia pp. 29–37; Peter Rosemann pp. 6–10, 12–13;
Published by Verlag Kettler, Dortmund, www.verlag-kettler.de

This catalogue is published on the occasion of the exhibition ... *these gestures of memory* by Gladys Kalichini, International Studio Programme, Künstlerhaus Bethanien, Berlin, June 19, 2020, to July 12, 2020. Gladys Kalichini is a grantholder of KfW Stiftung.

The artist would like to acknowledge: KfW Stiftung, Künstlerhaus Bethanien, The National Archives of Zambia, The National Archives of Zimbabwe, Post Studio Collective and The Arts of Africa and Global Souths Research Group. Sipho Banda, Deana and Shaun Brandon, Tomke Braun, Annet Busch, Noah Chanka, Alexander Akoto Danso, Marie-Hélène Gutberlet, Grace Kabungwe Kalichini, Leonard Kalichini, Monica Kalichini, Eric Kamau, Susan Kunju, Peju Layiwola, Daniela Leykam, Philiswa Lila, Bathandwa Makehle, Wallen Mapondera, Pamella Mqolweni, Fadzai Muchemwa, Andrew Mulenga, Victor Mutelekesha, Stary Mwaba, Claire Nalukenge, Bertina Nyalugwe, Valeria Schulte-Fischedick, Ruth Simbao

Pulications in this series so far: PARADISE / Thabiso Sekgala / January 2014, THE MADMAN SEES WHAT HE SEES / Carla Zaccagnini / March 2014, STORE IN A COOL AND DRY PLACE / Prajakta Potnis / November 2014, LIFE ON MARS / Stary Mwaba / March 2015, THE LAND BENEATH MY FEET / Khvay Samnang / September 2015, IN SILENCE / Nguyen Thi Thanh Mai / March 2016, INTENDING PROBABILITY / Salwa Aleryani / March 2017, AOS VENCEDORES AS BATATAS / Matheus Rocha Pitta / June 2017, EXIT – ENTRANCE / Orawan Arunrak / August 2017, ALL THAT IS SEEN AND UNSEEN / Vartan Avakian / January 2019 / FEEDING THE SCENE / Elia Nurvista / July 2019, RADIO CARABUCO / Andrés Pereira Paz / November 2019

KÜNSTLERHAUS BETHANIEN

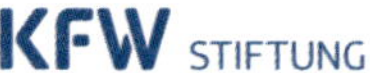